POSITIVE HEALTH GUIDE

THE DIABETICS' COOKBOOK

Delicious new recipes for entertaining and all the family

Roberta Longstaff, SRD, and Dr Jim Mann

Foreword by Dr Arnold Bloom, MD, FRCP
Executive Council Chairman,
British Diabetic Association

MARTIN DUNITZ

First published in the United Kingdom in 1984
by Martin Dunitz Ltd, 154 Camden High Street, London NW1 ONE.

British Library Cataloguing in Publication Data

Longstaff, Roberta
The diabetics' cookbook.–(Positive health guide)
1. Diabetics–Diet therapy–Recipes
I. Title II. Mann, Jim III. Series
641.5'6314 RC662

ISBN 0-906348-68-4
ISBN 0-906348-67-6 Pbk

Phototypeset by Book Ens, Saffron Walden, Essex

Printed by Toppan Printing Company (S) Pte Ltd, Singapore

Front cover photograph shows: Stuffed Rainbow Trout (top left, see p. 56), Fromage Blanc and Fruit (top right, see p. 86), Mushroom and Lentil Pâté (bottom left, see p. 21), Curried Chick Pea Salad (bottom right, see p. 28).

Back cover photograph shows: Neapolitan Pasta Salad (top left, see p. 30), Orange Sorbet Basket (top centre, see p. 77), Celebration Melon (top right, see p. 60), Kipper Pâté (bottom left, see p. 21), White Wine Cup (centre, see p. 68), Pork Kebabs (bottom right, see p. 58).

Roberta Longstaff, SRD, has worked as a nutritional adviser in industry and in hospitals, and was last appointed the post of Area Dietician for the Oxfordshire Area Health Authority. She remains a key member of Dr Mann's team, and has written all the recipes featured in *The Diabetics' Cookbook*. She has many years' experience of advising diabetics on their diet – many of her recipes being in fact derived from her patients' own most popular high-fibre cooking ideas. Roberta Longstaff has lived for a number of years in North America and the Far East, and now resides in Oxfordshire.

Dr Jim Mann is University Lecturer in Social and Community Medicine at Oxford University, and Honorary Consultant Physician at the Radcliffe Infirmary and John Radcliffe Hospital in Oxford.

Dr Mann is one of the world's leading diabetologists and over the last ten years has pioneered research into revolutionizing diabetic diets. Much of his research has involved the comparison of new high-fibre diets with the old-fashioned low-carbohydrate, high-fat diabetic diets. He and his team have confirmed the success of their new diet in controlling blood sugar by monitoring its effects over several years in large numbers of patients.

He runs a busy diabetic clinic in Oxford, plays an active role in the British Diabetic Association, has written numerous scientific papers and articles, and is renowned worldwide for his specialist lectures on diabetic diet.

FOREWORD

Dr Arnold Bloom MD, FRCP
Executive Council Chairman
British Diabetic Association

Eating the right food is of paramount importance for the future health of those with diabetes, especially as so much of the prepared food we buy today is laced with surplus sugar and fat.

Food should be enjoyed and this cookbook features recipes that are good for everybody, whether they have diabetes or not. Each recipe sets out the energy value, the proportions of carbohydrate, protein and fat and the fibre content of its components.

Nobody who takes an interest in cooking good food can fail to enjoy and gain benefit from this book.

CONTENTS

INTRODUCTION

Following the publication of our *Diabetics' Diet Book* in 1982, we have been overwhelmed by letters from a great number of people with diabetes; and it is in response to their enthusiasm that we have prepared this further collection of recipes. In the original book we explained in detail how the high-fibre, low-fat diet helps to control diabetes, and showed exactly how to change over to this new pattern of eating. This sequel volume is primarily designed to broaden the scope of modern diabetic cookery, not only by providing a wider range of wholesome everyday recipes, but also by introducing dinner and drinks party dishes, children's meals and food for festive occasions to the diabetic cook's repertoire.

Before we move on to the recipes, we want first to look briefly at the latest thinking on the benefits of our diet to diabetic health, and then to summarize the key points to remember when you are changing to our high-fibre eating programme.

Why high-fibre?

Until a few years ago, a reduction of all carbohydrate foods – both starchy (potatoes and cereals, for example) and sugary – was the mainstay of dietary advice to diabetics throughout the Western world. Such diets were quite often high in fat. Now, the national diabetic associations of Britain, the United States, Canada, Australia, Finland and several other Western countries recommend to insulin-dependent and non-insulin dependent diabetics the kind of diets we at Oxford have been studying and advising for a number of years – one which is high in fibre-rich carbohydrate and low in fat.

In brief, the advantages of a diet such as ours are as follows:

1. Reducing the amount of fat helps to lower blood cholesterol levels (which are often raised in people with diabetes) and so hopefully in the long run reduces the risk of heart attacks, to which diabetics are particularly prone.

2. Dietary fibre or roughage – in particular, fibre in various types of cooked dried beans (haricot, red kidney, soya beans, and lentils, for example) – helps to lower blood sugar levels towards normal. It is believed that blood sugar levels which are too high are associated with diabetic complications, such as recurrent infections and eye problems. So the likely benefits of keeping your blood sugar levels within normal limits are obvious.

3. Many non-insulin dependent diabetics are overweight and

need to lose weight to help control their condition. A high-fibre diet is filling, which helps make slimming easier.

The latest research
Since the publication of our first book, there have been several areas of research into diabetic diet.

Starchy foods Some researchers, including Prof David Jenkins in Toronto in 1983, have suggested recently that not all starchy carbohydrate foods are equally good. We stressed in *The Diabetics' Diet Book*, and do so again here, that the best sources of fibre are leguminous – such as in cooked dried beans; they are also a good source of protein. But we continue to believe that wholemeal bread, oats, wholegrain pasta, high-fibre sugar-free breakfast cereals, brown rice, potatoes (especially in their jackets) are good sources of carbohydrate for the diabetic.

Our continuing long-term studies in Oxford have shown a considerable improvement in diabetic control in people eating diets high in these foods. It is possible that further research will highlight some of these foods as being particularly beneficial, and indeed, even as far as legumes – or pulses – are concerned, some may be better than others. For the present, though, we recommend that you eat reasonable proportions of each of these foods.

Sugar Another recent controversial suggestion, made in 1983 by Dr Bantle in the United States, has been that under certain circumstances, sugar might be permissible for diabetics. This possibility has been based on a series of experimental breakfast meals in which different carbohydrates were given as part of mixed cooked breakfast. When sugar was given in this way, blood sugar levels did not appear to be higher than after the other starchy carbohydrates – none of which were particularly high in fibre.

The main criticism of this study is that it related to only one meal in the day. There are as yet no studies where sugar has been given to diabetics over a long period of time. In the future, it may prove to be possible for some diabetics, both insulin dependent and non-insulin dependent, who are not overweight to have a certain amount of sugar as part of their overall daily calorie intake. But we would strongly advise all diabetics *against* this practice at present until the results of longer-term studies are available. There are certainly some diabetics whose condition becomes appreciably worse when they add sugar to their diet.

Fat There's still not complete agreement among scientists about whether diabetics should be given any specific advice about the type of fat they should use, given that on the new calorie-controlled diet you have to reduce the amount of fat you eat because you are increasing the quantity of fibre-rich carbohydrate. With the notable exception of southern Europeans, most societies eating what is regarded as a typical Western diet have only a small proportion of their total fat intake from polyunsaturated sources, such as certain vegetable oils and margarine. Most experts now believe that polyunsaturated fat should provide at least half as many calories in your diet as saturated fat, the latter being contained in foods such as meat, lard and butter. In Britain today polyunsaturated fats provide only quarter, although in other Western countries such as the United States the ratio is somewhat higher. The reasons why you should increase the proportion of polyunsaturated fat are:

1. Polyunsaturated fat has a cholesterol lowering effect.
2. Polyunsaturated fat may confer some further benefit by reducing the risk of blood clotting in the arteries. Both of these effects help to protect against heart disease.

The recommended proportions of fat can be achieved by using polyunsaturated fat for spreading as well as for cooking wherever possible. We have adopted this approach in the recipes that follow, but we would remind you, as indicated in the golden rules below, that overall fat reduction is probably even more important than precisely what type of fat you eat.

The overall benefit of our diet In contrast to these areas of controversy there have been several studies since the publication of *The Diabetics' Diet Book*, from a number of European countries, which have confirmed the overall benefit of the high-fibre, low-fat eating plan.

Two new studies from Oxford are particularly interesting. One was carried out in 1982 by some of our colleagues who specialize in treating diabetes in children. This team, led by Dr Anne Louise Kinmonth, has shown that such a diet is acceptable and beneficial not only to adults but to diabetic children as well. In the light of this evidence we hope that our chapter of children's recipes will help parents to keep their children's condition under better control. In another study, carried out by Susan Lousley of our dietetic group in 1984, we recommended our high-fibre, low-fat diet to diabetics who were badly controlled on maximum doses of antidiabetes tablets, and as a result were being considered for further treatment by insulin injections. The great majority showed such an improvement that insulin was no longer considered necessary, and for some the dose of tablets was actually reduced. This last experiment is particularly important because it is one of the few where poorly controlled diabetics have been studied. Most other studies into the new diet have involved only relatively well-controlled diabetics.

How to use this book
We discussed dietary planning in detail in *The Diabetics' Diet Book*. If you intend to change over to high-fibre, low-fat eating we would advise you to refer to that book; and when converting to the new diet, it is, of course, essential to do so in consultation with your doctor or dietician.

You can, however, use the recipes in this book without needing our original volume. Because we have included comprehensive nutritional analyses with each recipe, they can be integrated into any high-fibre eating plan your doctor or dietician recommends.

Golden rules for healthy eating
There are three golden rules for all diabetics who intend to take their diet and diabetic control seriously, whether they need insulin injections or not.

1. Control your intake of calories in order to achieve or stay at your ideal body weight. For most diabetics this will involve a reduction of calories. If you are moderately overweight you will probably be able to reach your ideal weight by eating low-calorie foods and by concentrating on the low-calorie recipes given here and in *The Diabetics' Diet Book*.

If you are very overweight, you will only be able to achieve this by sticking to a planned daily calorie limit and counting the calories in all the food and drink you consume. Again, the previous book or your doctor or dietician will give you the information you need to do this. We have included five sample menu plans at the end of this book which suggest how you can fit our recipes into different daily calorie levels.

2. Eat more high-fibre foods (such as pulses, wholemeal cereals, pasta and brown rice, fruit and vegetables), less fat (lard, oils and butter, for example) and less quickly absorbed sugar (found in sweet cakes, chocolates and so on).

Use as many as possible of our specially created high-fibre, low-fat recipes. Have two slices of wholemeal bread every day and a substantial helping of cooked dried beans, or a recipe containing them, daily or at least several times a week.

Carbohydrate counting, which is necessary for all insulin-dependent and some non-insulin dependent diabetics, is described fully in *The Diabetics' Diet Book*.

3. Eat regular meals This is a sensible practice for diabetics and non-diabetics alike. However, balancing insulin with food is essential if you take insulin and wish to achieve good control – for you, regular meals are essential.

We hope that the following recipes will help to make the high-fibre, low-fat diet an enjoyable way of eating. We have found that most diabetics who become accustomed to it far prefer it to the traditional Western diet they had been eating before. Please remind your families that it is a far healthier way of life for non-diabetics as well. Our hope is that diabetics will lead the way to healthier eating for the entire population.

THE RECIPES: Useful information

Weights and measures

In all the recipes, calculations are based on metric weights and measures, but wherever practical these have been expressed in household measures or descriptions. Where this is not possible the nearest equivalent in Imperial weights (pounds and ounces) has been given.

The tablespoon measurement used throughout the book equals 15 ml and the teaspoon 5 ml; both are level unless otherwise stated. Check the size of your spoons to ensure success.

Australian users should remember that as their tablespoon has been converted to 20 ml, and is therefore larger than the tablespoon measurement used in the recipes in this book, they should use 3 × 5 ml tsp where instructed to use 1 × 15 ml tbsp.

Changing the quantities

The quantities used in most of the recipes can be halved to accommodate the smaller family. Where only a single serving is required, the remainder can usually be reheated a day or two later or deep-frozen. Casserole-type recipes are particularly good for reheating.

Calories and joules

The kilocalorie (kcal), expressed in the original *Diabetics' Diet Book* as Calories or Cals for short, is used to express the energy content of food. The metric equivalent – kilojoule (kJ) – is also given. Carbohydrate has been rounded off to the nearest 10 g and is also given in units, each equalling 10 g. If below 5 g, the carbohydrate value is stated as negligible. Fibre, protein and fat values have been rounded to the nearest gram.

Ingredients

We recommend that you use the following ingredients in your cooking:

- Wholemeal (also called wholewheat) breads, flours and pastas; brown rice and pulses.

- When buying wholemeal flour, make sure it is 100 per cent – that is, unrefined.
- Skimmed milk or reconstituted dried skimmed milk.
- Cheeses made from skimmed milk such as cottage cheese and quark (or quarg) and curd cheeses (provided they are labelled as low fat).
- Try the new range of stirred yoghurts classified as very low fat (0.3 per cent). The calories are lower than in any other yoghurts (48 kcal in 100 g). They are described as 'waistline' and come in natural and fruit flavours.
- Polyunsaturated margarines and low-fat spreads and polyunsaturated oils, such as corn, soya or sunflower.
- Fish and meat low in fat (with all visible fat trimmed from meat).
- Chicken can always be substituted for turkey if it is easier or more economical.
- Fresh fruit and vegetables with the skins left on, if possible. Frozen and canned may be substituted, but check that sugar has not been added.
- Herbs and spices – these are always a matter of personal preference and the amounts can be adjusted to suit individual tastes. The quantities given are usually for fresh herbs; frozen herbs are the best alternative, but if using dried herbs, use about ⅓ of the amount stated.
- Sugar substitutes: sweeteners should be sugar-free. The amounts used may be varied to suit individual tastes.

Useful food to keep in the refrigerator

- Prepared summer and winter salad vegetables. Store, covered in plastic containers.
- Yoghurt, fresh fruit, fruit juice
- Skimmed-milk quark or cottage cheese
- Low-fat salad dressings (see pages 101–2)
- Fresh vegetables which can be quickly cooked, such as tomatoes and peppers (they are good sources of vitamin C)
- Cooked beans and brown rice.

Cooking and preparation

- Grill, bake, steam, poach or boil in place of frying.
- Glaze pies with skimmed milk instead of egg and milk.
- Make sauces by blending the thickening agent with the liquid and bring to the boil, stirring, rather than by melting the fat, adding the thickener and making a roux.
- When making wholemeal pastry a good way of overcoming the problem of making holes in the dough when rolling it out is to

roll it between sheets of polythene or greaseproof paper.
- Wholemeal flours vary in the amount of liquid they will absorb, so in baking add 1–2 tbsp extra water if the consistency is too stiff. Where self-raising wholemeal flour is stated in a plain cake-mixture, 1 tsp baking powder per 100 g/3½ oz unrefined wholemeal flour may be used instead.
- In recipes which feature stock you can use stock cubes if you don't have home-made stock. Where the stock flavour is not specified, use whichever you like.
- All soups will keep for two days in a refrigerator.
- Seasoning with salt should be light.

Cooking equipment
- Use good-quality non-stick pans, casseroles and baking dishes to reduce cooking oil and fat to a minimum. Other baking dishes can be lined with non-stick paper.
- When baking larger pieces of meat and some vegetables, use roasting bags or foil covering to retain the juices and keep the food tender.
- Using an electric blender for processing food is better than sieving, because it ensures that valuable fibre remains in the food. Do not blend food to too fine a purée. If you use a Mouli-mill or other type of sieve instead of a blender, make sure no fibre-rich residue remains in the utensil.
- Shop around for a clay pot suitable for cooking jacket potatoes on a gas ring.
- Use a Continental cheese slicer to make wafer-thin slivers of hard cheese.
- Perforated cooking spoons are recommended, as they help to drain off the fat used in cooking.

Pulses
Many supermarkets now stock a wide variety of dried, frozen and canned pulses and the unusual types can be found in Oriental food shops, delicatessens and health-food stores.

Canned beans may replace cooked beans in recipes, providing no sugar has been used in canning.

You can vary the type of beans specified in the recipes without significantly affecting the analyses – except with soya beans which have different dietary constituents.

Soaking Wash thoroughly and soak in cold water overnight. Alternatively, place in a pan of cold water, bring to the boil and cook for 2–3 minutes. Remove from the heat, cover and leave to soak for 1 hour. The weight of the soaked beans is about double their dry weight. In the recipes, where the bean weights are expressed as: a certain amount, soaked, this is the weight before soaking – in other words, the dry weight. Cooked beans weigh approximately double their dry weight.

Cooking Put the beans in a large pan with plenty of water. Boil rapidly for 10 minutes. Cover and simmer gently until soft, stirring occasionally to ensure even cooking. The cooking time varies according to the type and even those of the same type can take different times, depending on their age and the amount being cooked. If you cook pulses frequently, you may consider it worth while buying a pressure-cooker as this reduces the cooking times.

Many of the smaller varieties, lentils and aduki beans, for example, can be cooked without soaking, but allow a little longer for cooking.

up to 30 minutes (*10 minutes in pressure-cooker*):	aduki beans British field beans mung beans peas split peas split red lentils
30 minutes to 1 hour (*15–20 minutes in pressure-cooker*):	black-eyed beans black beans barlotti beans cannellini beans flageolot beans Continental lentils ful madames lima beans
1 to 2 hours (*½–1 hour in pressure-cooker*):	broad beans butter beans chick peas haricot beans speckled Mexican beans red kidney beans
3 to 4 hours (*1–1½ hours in pressure-cooker*):	soya beans

Leave the seasoning until cooking is almost complete, as the addition of salt, vinegar, lemon juice or tomatoes tends to toughen the skin and prevent cooking.

Cooked beans are versatile: they will keep in the refrigerator for 3–4 days, or for a month or more in the deep-freeze if mixed with onions, etc (or a year if cooked alone). Many bean dishes can be reheated and served again.

To save time and energy, cook larger quantities than stated in the recipes and use leftovers later for quick snacks, soups, salads and so on. Herbs and spices can be varied and different sauces added, such as Worcester, soya, low-calorie ketchup and salad dressings. Beans can also be heated through in home-made sauces (see pages 98–100) and served with brown rice, wholemeal pasta or on wholemeal toast, with added fresh vegetables or accompanied by other vegetable dishes.

Brown rice

There are three principal varieties of brown rice. Long grain e.g. Patna – the grains remain separate and fluff up when cooked. It is used to accompany savoury dishes or it may form part of the dish. Round or short grain – is used for making rice puddings as the grains are inclined to become sticky and clump together when cooked. Medium grain rice with rounded ends – varieties grown in Italy and Spain are used for making risotto and paella, but are difficult to find elsewhere. Substitute with long grain brown rice, if necessary.

Brown rice has more flavour than white rice, and has a higher vitamin and mineral content, although the B vitamin, Thiamin, needed by the body to utilize carbohydrate will be lost in the cooking water unless the correct proportions of rice to liquid are used. These are – 1 measure of rice to 2 measures of boiling water and 1 tsp of salt per 600 ml/1 pt water or stock.

Cooking Bring the measured amount of water to the boil, add the rice (washed, if necessary) and salt, return to simmering point. Stir once, cover tightly and simmer steadily for about 40 minutes or until the grains are just tender.

Leave alone when cooking – if the lid is lifted, steam will escape and slow down the cooking time and, if stirred, the grains will break releasing the starch inside, making the rice sticky and lumpy.

If the water has not been completely absorbed, leave uncovered over the heat for a few minutes.

Cooked rice can then be gently fluffed up with a fork, or copy the Chinese and leave the rice tightly covered on the lowest possible heat for 10 minutes. It is a great advantage to have a heavy pan for this.

If there are cooking instructions on the packet, follow them: some varieties of brown rice require more than twice the quantity of water to rice.

Cooking in the oven Use the same proportions of rice to water. Put the rice and salt in a casserole, stir in the boiling water and cook in the oven for approximately 1–1¼ hours at 180°C/350°F/gas 4.

Reheating It is often convenient to cook a larger quantity than required – covered, it will keep in the refrigerator for a week. To reheat, place in a pan with a little water and put over a gentle heat, giving an occasional stir, or place in an ovenproof dish with a little water, cover tightly and heat in the oven for about 20 minutes.

Wholemeal pasta
There are about a dozen varieties of plain wholemeal pasta shapes. They can be bought in supermarkets, country stores and healthfood stores.

Wholemeal pasta is suitable to include in your diet as it is high in carbohydrate, low in fat and has a good fibre content. It has more flavour and a firmer texture than ordinary pasta.

Pasta can be treated/used as a main course or snack meal, or used in place of potatoes to accompany meat and fish dishes. It is also delicious in soups or cooked and added to salads. Try serving pasta with some of the sauces on pages 98–100.

Cooking If there are cooking instructions on the packet it is wise to follow them. Allow plenty of boiling water to prevent the pasta sticking together: approximately 4 litres (6–8 pints) water for each 450 g/1 lb pasta. Slowly add the pasta to the boiling water so that the water does not go off the boil. Stir with a fork to ensure it does not stick together or to the pan, and cook steadily, uncovered, until just tender, but still firm. The cooking time will vary from approximately 8–18 minutes depending on the size and freshness of the pasta. Drain well.

SOUPS AND STARTERS

LIGHT SOUPS

Leek and potato soup

Serves 4
Each serving: 150 kcal/630 kJ, 20 g (2 units) carbohydrate, 6 g fibre, 7 g protein, 3 g fat

8 young leeks
2 medium-sized potatoes (with skin)
1 tbsp polyunsaturated margarine
600 ml/1 pt chicken stock
onion salt
pepper
300 ml/½ pt skimmed milk
2 tbsp chopped chives
2 tbsp chopped parsley

Roughly chop the leeks and potatoes and place in a saucepan with the margarine and a few spoonfuls of stock. Stir well, then cover with a tight-fitting lid and simmer gently for about 20 minutes to let the flavours sweat into the liquid. Give the pan an occasional shake. Add the remaining stock and seasoning to the vegetables, replace the lid and continue cooking for a further 10 minutes or until the vegetables are cooked.

Remove from the heat, add the milk and purée in a blender. Return to the rinsed saucepan and reheat gently. Adjust the seasoning and stir in the chives and parsley just before serving.

Rice, corn and carrot broth

Serves 4
Each serving: 120 kcal/500 kJ, 20 g (2 units) carbohydrate, 3 g fibre, 6 g protein, 1 g fat

1 medium-sized onion, chopped
850 ml/1½ pt beef or lamb stock
celery salt
pepper
2 tbsp long- or short-grain brown rice
1 medium-sized carrot, diced
5 tbsp dried skimmed milk
200 ml/⅓ pt stock
few drops tabasco sauce
150 g/5 oz fresh or frozen sweetcorn kernels
2 tbsp chopped parsley

Put the onion, meat stock and seasoning into a large saucepan, cover and bring to the boil. Add the rice and boil gently for 30 minutes. Stir in the carrot and continue cooking for a further 15–20 minutes. Blend the milk with the remaining stock and tabasco and stir into the soup along with the sweetcorn kernels. Garnish with parsley before serving.

Spinach soup

See page 26

Serves 4

Each serving: 200 kcal/840 kJ, 20 g (2 units) carbohydrate, 12 g fibre, 18 g protein, 6 g fat

15 g/½ oz polyunsaturated margarine
1 small onion, chopped
2 rashers lean bacon, finely chopped
300 g/10½ oz frozen chopped spinach
seasoning
600 ml/1 pt skimmed milk
1 chicken stock cube, crumbled
good pinch grated nutmeg
100 g/3½ oz sliced wholemeal bread, toasted
paprika

Melt the margarine in a saucepan. Add the onion and bacon and cook gently for 10 minutes, stirring occasionally. Add the spinach (in frozen state), stirring well and breaking down with a spoon. Add the seasoning, cover and simmer gently, giving the pan an occasional shake, until the spinach is soft.

Purée in a blender along with a little of the milk, return to the rinsed pan and stir in the remainder of the milk and the stock cube. Heat through, stirring occasionally. Dice the toast into small croûtons, toss in paprika and serve with the soup. On special occasions garnish with a slice of lemon dotted with paprika.

Vegetable and wholemeal pasta broth

Serves 4

Each serving: 100 kcal/420 kJ, 20 g (2 units) carbohydrate, 6 g fibre, 8 g protein, 1 g fat

2 medium-sized onions, chopped
1 large leaf of spinach (with veins), finely chopped
2 medium-sized leeks, very finely chopped
850 ml/1½ pt stock
45 g/1½ oz wholemeal pasta shapes
seasoning
60 g/2 oz lean ham, finely diced
2 tbsp chopped chives
pinch grated nutmeg

Place the onions, spinach and leeks in a saucepan with the stock, cover and bring to the boil. Sprinkle in the pasta and seasoning and simmer for 20 minutes. Stir in the ham and simmer for a further 10 minutes. Add the chives and nutmeg, adjust the seasoning if necessary and serve.

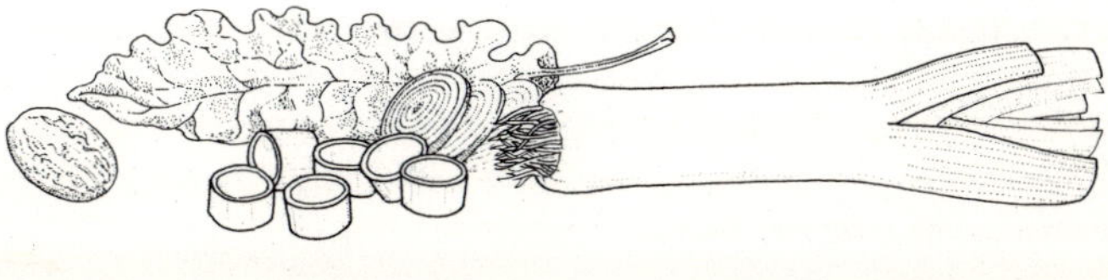

MAIN COURSE SOUPS

Canadian fish chowder

Serves 4
Each serving: 310 kcal/1300 kJ, 40 g (4 units) carbohydrate, 5 g fibre, 23 g protein, 10 g fat

1 tbsp polyunsaturated oil
*600 ml/1 pt strong fish stock**
1 rasher streaky bacon, chopped
2 small onions, chopped
2 medium-sized potatoes (with skin), diced
celery salt
pepper
300 g/10½ oz white fish trimmings, cut into small pieces
300 g/10½ oz fresh or frozen sweetcorn kernels
300 ml/½ pt skimmed milk
1 tbsp Worcester sauce
4 tbsp chopped parsley
paprika

Heat the oil with a few spoonfuls of stock and cook the bacon, onions and potatoes for about 5 minutes or until lightly browned. Cover and simmer over low heat for 10 minutes. Add the remaining stock and seasoning and bring to the boil. Stir in the fish and sweetcorn and simmer gently for 10 minutes. Add the milk and bring to the boil again. Adjust the seasoning and stir in the Worcester sauce and parsley. Sprinkle with paprika before serving.

Other scraps of fish – clams, crabmeat and lobster may be substituted for the white fish.

Chicken and celery soup

Serves 4, twice
Each serving: 100 kcal/420 kJ, 10 g (1 unit) carbohydrate, 3 g fibre, 9 g protein, 2 g fat

500 g/18 oz celery stalks
1 medium-sized potato
1 large spring onion
200 g/7 oz chicken meat
850 ml/1½ pt chicken stock
seasoning
300 ml/½ pt skimmed milk
115 g/4 oz sliced wholemeal bread, toasted

Roughly cut up the vegetables and chicken. Put into a saucepan with the stock and seasoning, and cook gently until all are tender. Add the milk, then purée in a blender. Return to the rinsed saucepan and reheat until hot.

Dice the toast into croûtons and serve with the soup.

---

*Made from simmering skin, bones and heads of fish with a few parsley stalks and a small bay leaf for 20 minutes. Strain well before using.

Bean and vegetable soup

Serves 4, twice

Each serving: 200 kcal/840 kJ, 30 g (3 units) carbohydrate, 16 g fibre, 13 g protein, 5 g fat

2 tbsp polyunsaturated oil
2 litres/3½ pt stock
2 medium-sized carrots, diced
2 medium-sized leeks or onions, sliced
2 stalks celery, sliced
400 g/14 oz haricot beans, soaked (see pages 12–13)
6–8 bacon rinds or a ham bone, cracked
4 tsp chopped thyme, or 2 tsp dried thyme
seasoning
2 tbsp Worcester sauce (optional)
skimmed milk (optional, not included in calculation)
4 tbsp chopped parsley

Heat the oil with a few spoonfuls of stock and gently cook the carrots, leeks and celery for about 20 minutes, stirring occasionally. Add the beans, bacon rinds or ham bone, the remaining stock and thyme, and bring to the boil. Simmer for 2–2½ hours, skimming the surface occasionally, or until the beans are tender. Season to taste and remove the bacon rinds or bone.

Serve the soup as a broth or purée in a blender, but do not blend too finely: leave some pieces of coloured vegetable visible. Add Worcester sauce and skimmed milk, if using, and stir in the chopped parsley. Serve at once.

Note

Other varieties of beans, peas or lentils may be substituted for the haricot beans, in which case adjust cooking times from information on page 13.

Four-bean pasta soup

See page 26

Serves 4 (twice)

Each serving: 170 kcal/710 kJ, 30 g (3 units) carbohydrate, 13 g fibre, 12 g protein, 1 g fat

200 g/7 oz fresh or frozen runner beans, chopped
200 g/7 oz fresh or frozen broad beans
3 medium-sized leeks, finely chopped
2 litres/3½ pt meat or chicken stock
1 tbsp tomato purée
200 g/7 oz cooked red kidney beans (see pages 12–13)
200 g/7 oz cooked haricot beans (see pages 12–13)
garlic salt
pepper
125 g/4½ oz wholemeal pasta rollers (or other small shapes)
bouquet garni (parsley, bay leaf and thyme or other favourite herbs)
2 tbsp chopped parsley

Put the runner beans, broad beans, leeks and stock into a saucepan and simmer for about 10 minutes. Add the tomato purée, kidney beans, haricot beans and seasoning, and bring to the boil. Sprinkle in the pasta and bouquet garni and simmer gently for a further 15 minutes or until the pasta is tender.

Just before serving, adjust the seasoning, remove the bouquet garni and stir in the parsley.

Scottish lentil broth

Serves 4, twice

Each serving: 190 kcal/800 kJ, 40 g (4 units) carbohydrate, 9 g fibre, 14 g protein, negligible fat

400 g/14 oz red lentils
2 litres/3½ pt water
1 ham bone, cracked or about 8 bacon rinds
2 medium-sized carrots, diced
1 medium-sized onion, chopped
1 medium-sized leek, chopped
200 g/7 oz cabbage, finely shredded
1 medium–large potato, diced
1 bouquet garni (parsley, bay leaf and thyme)
seasoning
4 tbsp chopped parsley

Put the lentils, water and ham bone into a large saucepan. Bring to the boil and boil for 10 minutes. Reduce the heat to low and simmer for 20 minutes. Stir in the vegetables, bouquet garni and seasoning, return to the boil and simmer for about 30 minutes or until all of the vegetables are cooked. Remove the ham bone and bouquet garni. Stir in the parsley, adjust the seasoning if necessary and serve.

Alternatively, this soup may be put through a blender, but do not blend too finely.

Note

Soaked brown lentils, dried beans or peas may be substituted for red lentils. Adjust cooking times from information on page 13.

STARTERS

Seafood pâté

See page 26

Each 30 g/1 oz: 25 kcal/100 kJ, negligible (0 units) carbohydrate, 1 g fibre, 4 g protein, negligible fat

225 g/8 oz poached smoked haddock fillets, skinned, boned and flaked
200 g/7 oz cooked white beans, mashed (see pages 12–13)
4 tbsp skimmed milk curd cheese
1 tsp anchovy essence
1 tbsp lemon juice
2 drops tabasco sauce

Mash the haddock, beans and cheese together, then thoroughly mix in the remaining ingredients; or purée all the ingredients together in a blender. Spoon into a serving dish or small pots. Store in the refrigerator until ready to serve. Eat within 2 days.

For special occasions, parsley, strips of anchovy fillets, shrimps and slices of lemon may be used to garnish.

To make a softer pâté, add a little liquid from cooking the fish or beans and use as a sandwich spread, toast topper or for canapés.

Kipper pâté

Each 30 g/1 oz: 30 kcal/130 kJ, negligible (0 units) carbohydrate, 1 g fibre, 4 g protein, 1 g fat

250 g/9 oz poached kipper fillets, skinned, boned and flaked
4 tbsp skimmed milk curd cheese
200 g/7 oz cooked white beans, mashed (see pages 12–13)
1 tbsp lemon juice
2 tsp anchovy essence
pinch cayenne pepper
pepper

Mash the kipper and cheese together, then thoroughly mix in the remaining ingredients; or purée all the ingredients together in a blender. Adjust the seasoning. Spoon into a serving dish or small pots, cover and store in the refrigerator until ready to serve. Serve with hot wholemeal toast, or use as a sandwich spread, toast topper or for canapés. May be garnished with prawns (not included in analysis), cucumber and parsley.

Mushroom and lentil pâté

Each 30 g/1 oz: 20 kcal/80 kJ, negligible (0 units) carbohydrate, 1 g fibre, 1 g protein, 1 g fat

1 small onion, finely chopped
1 tsp polyunsaturated oil
200 g/7 oz flat mushrooms
100 g/3½ oz cooked brown lentils (see pages 12–13)
60 g/2 oz skimmed milk curd cheese
2 tbsp chopped parsley
1 tbsp lemon juice
garlic salt
pepper
3 tbsp canned consommé (optional)

Cook the onion in the oil in a non-stick pan until soft. Grill the mushrooms for 2 minutes under a medium grill. Add all the remaining ingredients and purée together in a blender. Spoon into a serving dish or small pots, cover and store in the refrigerator until firm. Serve as pâté accompanied by lettuce, tomato and cucumber, or use as a sandwich spread, toast topper or for canapés. May be garnished with mushrooms, watercress and tomato.

SALADS

MAIN COURSE SALADS

Rollmop herrings with potato salad

Serves 4
Each serving: 300 kcal/1260 kJ, 30 g (3 units) carbohydrate, 9 g fibre, 19 g protein, 12 g fat

8 small rollmops or soused herrings
2 tbsp chopped chives
200 g/7 oz boiled potatoes, diced
400 g/14 oz cooked haricot beans (see pages 12–13)
150 ml/¼ pt Green Dressing (see page 102)
½ medium-sized cucumber, with skin, diced
2 medium-sized tomatoes, quartered

Cut the herrings into thin strips, place in the centre of a serving dish and sprinkle with chives. Combine the potatoes and beans, pour over the dressing and mix gently. Arrange around the outside of the serving dish and sprinkle with the cucumber. Place the tomatoes, skin side up, between the herrings and the border.

Ham and aduki bean salad

Serves 4
Each serving: 150 kcal/630 kJ, 10 g (1 unit) carbohydrate, 8 g fibre, 15 g protein, 4 g fat

1 large lettuce
100 g/3½ oz cooked lean ham, chopped
200 g/7 oz cooked aduki beans (see pages 12–13)
1 large bunch watercress
8 small tomatoes
2 hard-boiled eggs, quartered lengthways

Dressing
4 tbsp tomato juice
1 tbsp Worcester sauce
1 tbsp finely chopped onion
seasoning

Arrange a nest of lettuce leaves in a large salad bowl or dish. Combine the dressing ingredients together then stir in the ham and beans. Put the mixture into the bowl or dish. Place sprigs of watercress between the meat mixture and the lettuce. Garnish with quartered tomatoes and eggs.

OPPOSITE: Coleslaw with Carrot and Sultanas (top, see p. 29), Ham and Aduki Bean Salad (centre), Rollmop Herrings with Potato Salad (bottom). OVERLEAF: Stuffed Aubergines and Tomato Sauce (top left, see p. 32), Tuscan Beans with Pasta (top right, see p. 37), Spanish Rice (bottom left, see p. 38), Dieters' Ratatouille (bottom right, see p. 32).

Tuna, chick pea and pasta salad

Serves 4
Each serving: 210 kcal/880 kJ, 30 g (3 units) carbohydrate, 16 g fibre, 15 g protein, 3 g fat

300 g/10½ oz cooked chick peas (see pages 12–13)
200 g/7 oz cooked wholemeal pasta shapes (see page 15)
6 large spring onions, chopped
2 tbsp finely chopped parsley
1 clove garlic, crushed
100 g/3½ oz canned tuna fish in brine, drained
6 tbsp Basic Yoghurt Dressing (see page 101)
lettuce leaves
1 tbsp dried mixed peppers, reconstituted

Combine the peas, pasta, spring onions, parsley and garlic. Mash the tuna with a fork and add the dressing, mixing them together thoroughly until smooth. Pour over the pea mixture and toss well. Allow to marinate together for 20–30 minutes, then serve on a bed of lettuce with the peppers sprinkled over the pea mixture.

Lentil and garlic salad

Serves 4
Each serving: 220 kcal/920 kJ, 30 g (3 units) carbohydrate, 9 g fibre, 15 g protein, 4 g fat

200 g/7 oz whole lentils
6 tbsp bottled low-calorie vinaigrette dressing
1 clove garlic, crushed
4 spring onions, chopped
4 medium-sized tomatoes, chopped
2 stalks celery, chopped
2 tbsp chopped parsley
seasoning
crisp lettuce leaves
30 g/1 oz black olives, quartered and stoned
1 hard-boiled egg, chopped

Cook lentils (see pages 12–13). Mix with dressing and garlic while still hot and leave to cool. Add remaining ingredients and mix well. Place on lettuce leaves and garnish with olives and egg.

Piquant pasta shell salad

Serves 4
Each serving: 310 kcal/1300 kJ, 50 g (5 units) carbohydrate, 13 g fibre, 16 g protein, 5 g fat

200 g/7 oz wholemeal pasta shells
5 tbsp Piquant Dressing (page 102)
1 clove garlic, crushed
200 g/7 oz red kidney beans canned without sugar, or cooked beans (see pages 12–13)
lettuce leaves
60 g/2 oz Continental smoked sausage, very finely chopped
4 medium-sized tomatoes, chopped ➧

Spinach Soup (top, see p. 17), Four-Bean Pasta Soup (bottom left, see p. 19), Seafood Pâté (see p. 20).

Cook the pasta in boiling salted water (see page 15). Drain and immediately toss in the Piquant Dressing and crushed garlic. Mix in the beans and leave to become really cold. Serve on a bed of lettuce leaves garnished with the sausage and tomatoes.

Curried chick pea salad

Serves 4

Each serving: 380 kcal/1600 kJ, 70 g (7 units) carbohydrate, 18 g fibre, 18 g protein, 5 g fat

100 g/3½ oz long-grain brown rice
250 ml/9 fl oz boiling chicken stock
1 tsp salt
60 g/2 oz fresh or frozen sweetcorn kernels, cooked
60 g/2 oz fresh or frozen peas, cooked
60 g/2 oz raisins, chopped
1 green apple, with skin, diced
1 tbsp lemon juice
150 ml/¼ pt Curry Yoghurt Dressing (see page 102)
1 tbsp Tomato Chutney (see page 101)
450 g/1 lb chick peas canned without sugar, or cooked chick peas (see pages 12–13)
2 small green peppers, cut into rings
1 hard-boiled egg, chopped or sliced

Cook the rice in the boiling salted stock (see page 14). Add the sweetcorn, peas and raisins and set aside to cool. Dip the apple in the lemon juice and mix into the cooled rice. Arrange in a border around the edge of a serving dish. Mix the curry yoghurt dressing with the chutney then fold in the chick peas. Pile the mixture into the centre of the dish and garnish with peppers and hard-boiled egg. Serve with a green salad.

Chicken or turkey and pasta salad

Serves 4

Each serving: 260 kcal/1090 kJ, 30 g (3 units) carbohydrate, 8 g fibre, 19 g protein, 7 g fat

100 g/3½ oz wholemeal pasta shells or rings
1 tbsp polyunsaturated oil
3 tbsp lemon juice
pinch grated nutmeg
seasoning
200 g/7 oz cooked chicken or turkey, diced
1 medium-sized red pepper, cut into strips
200 g/7 oz cooked haricot beans (see pages 12–13)
100 g/3½ oz sweetcorn kernels, cooked
2 tbsp chopped parsley or mixed fresh herbs
100 g/3½ oz endive or crisp lettuce leaves

Cook the pasta in boiling salted water (see page 15). Drain and toss in the oil and lemon juice. Cover and set aside to cool. Mix in the remaining ingredients except the endive leaves. Line a shallow serving dish with the endive and pile the salad on top.

ACCOMPANIMENT SALADS

Brown rice and sweetcorn salad

Serves 4
Each serving: 190 kcal/380 kJ, 30 g (3 units) carbohydrate, 7 g fibre, 5 g protein, 6 g fat

225 g/8 oz cooked long-grain brown rice (see page 14)
200 g/7 oz cooked sweetcorn kernels
4 tbsp natural bran flakes
1 small bunch spring onions, chopped
1 small red pepper, cut into rings

Dressing
1 tbsp polyunsaturated oil
1 tbsp wine vinegar
1 tbsp lemon juice
1 tsp Worcester sauce
½ tsp garlic salt
pepper

Combine the rice, sweetcorn and bran. Combine the dressing ingredients together then stir into the rice mixture. Sprinkle the spring onions and red pepper slices over the top, cover and set aside in a cool place for about 30 minutes before serving.

Coleslaw

Serves 4
Each serving: 30 kcal/130 kJ, negligible (0 units) carbohydrate, 2 g fibre, 2 g protein, negligible fat

225 g/8 oz crisp white cabbage heart, shredded
4 tbsp finely chopped onion
60 g/2 oz green pepper, chopped
4 tbsp Basic Yoghurt Dressing (see page 101)
seasoning

Mix all the ingredients together and season to taste.

Coleslaw with apple

Serves 4
Each serving: 40 kcal/170 kJ, 10 g (1 unit) carbohydrate, 2 g fibre, 2 g protein, negligible fat

As Coleslaw above, but add 1 average-sized crisp, tart eating apple, chopped.

Coleslaw with carrot and sultanas

Serves 4 See page 23
Each serving: 70 kcal/290 kJ, 10 g (1 unit) carbohydrate, 4 g fibre, 3 g protein, negligible fat

As Coleslaw, but add 1 fairly small carrot, grated and 60 g/2 oz sultanas, chopped.

Potato salad

Serves 4

Each serving: 100 kcal/420 kJ, 20 g (2 units) carbohydrate, 1 g fibre, 1 g protein, negligible fat

450 g/1 lb cooked potatoes, diced
4 tbsp Basic Yoghurt Dressing (see page 101)
1 tbsp finely chopped onion
1 tbsp chopped parsley

Use waxy potatoes if possible. Mix the cold potatoes with the dressing, onion and chopped parsley. Serve.

Potato and bean salad

Serves 4

Each serving: 110 kcal/460 kJ, 20 g (2 units) carbohydrate, 5 g fibre, 5 g protein, negligible fat

As Potato Salad above, but using 225 g/8 oz cooked haricot beans (see pages 12–13) and 225 g/8 oz cooked potato.

Neapolitan pasta salad

Serves 4

Each serving: 240 kcal/1010 kJ, 40 g (4 units) carbohydrate, 7 g fibre, 9 g protein, 5 g fat

250 g/9 oz wholemeal pasta shapes
1 bunch watercress or crisp lettuce leaves
6 black olives, halved and stoned
2 tbsp chopped chives

Tomato dressing
4 tbsp sugar-free tomato juice
1 tbsp wine vinegar
2 tsp sunflower or other polyunsaturated oil
1 tsp chopped basil or to taste
1 tsp chopped oregano or to taste
1 tbsp chopped parsley
garlic salt
pepper

Cook the pasta in boiling salted water (see page 15). Drain.

Meanwhile, mix the ingredients for the dressing together, pour over the hot pasta, toss well and leave to cool thoroughly. Line a salad bowl with watercress or lettuce leaves, pile the pasta in the centre and scatter the olives and chives over the top.

VEGETABLE DISHES

MAIN COURSE

Stuffed courgettes

Serves 4
Each serving: 180 kcal/760 kJ, 20 g (2 units) carbohydrate, 10 g fibre, 16 g protein, 4 g fat

2 medium–large courgettes
100 g/3½ oz onion, finely chopped
4 small, thin-cut slices wholemeal bread, crumbed
200 g/7 oz mushrooms, chopped
200 g/7 oz cooked haricot, or other, beans (see pages 12–13), chopped
4 tbsp chopped parsley
1 tsp beef extract dissolved in 2 tbsp boiling water
½ tsp dried basil
1 clove garlic, crushed
200 g/7 oz cottage cheese
seasoning
2 tbsp grated Parmesan or other strong cheese
paprika
sprigs of watercress

Heat the oven to 190°C/375°F/gas 5.

Cut the courgettes in half lengthways and scoop out the pulp. Dice. Mix the diced pulp with all the other ingredients except the Parmesan cheese, paprika and watercress. Pile into the courgette shells and place in a non-stick baking dish. Sprinkle with the Parmesan cheese and bake in the oven for 25–30 minutes or until tender and lightly browned. Sprinkle with paprika and garnish with watercress before serving.

Stuffed potatoes

Serves 4
Each serving: 250 kcal/1050 kJ, 40 g (4 units) carbohydrate, 5 g fibre, 14 g protein, 4 g fat

4 potatoes, each 200 g/7 oz
6 rashers lean bacon
8 tbsp Piquant Dressing (see page 102)
4 tbsp chopped parsley

Heat the oven to 200°C/400°F/gas 6.

Put the potatoes into the oven and bake until tender. Grill the bacon rashers until crisp, then chop. Cut the cooked potatoes in half and scoop out the centres. Mix the bacon, sauce and half the parsley with the potato flesh and pile the mixture back into the potato cases. Return the 8 cases to the oven for 10–15 minutes to heat through. Garnish with the remaining chopped parsley.

Stuffed aubergines and tomato sauce

Serves 4 or 8 See pages 24–5

Each filled half aubergine (serving 8): 100 kcal/420 kJ, 10 g (1 unit) carbohydrate, 5 g fibre, 5 g protein, 4 g fat

4 medium–small aubergines
1 tbsp polyunsaturated oil
2 medium-sized onions, chopped
1 clove garlic, crushed
100 g/3½ oz mushrooms, chopped
200 g/7 oz cooked soya splits or beans (see pages 12–13)
60 g/2 oz wholemeal breadcrumbs
4 tbsp chopped parsley
½ tsp ground mace
seasoning
300 ml/½ pt Tomato Sauce (see pages 100–1)

Heat the oven to 190°C/375°F/gas 5.

Cut the aubergines in half lengthways and scoop out the flesh, leaving a 5 mm/¼ in shell. Sprinkle the shells and flesh with salt and leave for 30 minutes, then rinse thoroughly and dry with kitchen paper. Chop the flesh.

Heat the oil. Add the onions and garlic and fry gently for 5 minutes until transparent. Add the aubergine flesh and mushrooms and continue to cook for a further 5 minutes, stirring occasionally. Transfer to a mixing bowl containing the bean splits, and mash the ingredients thoroughly together. Mix in the breadcrumbs, parsley, mace and seasoning. Place the aubergine shells in a non-stick baking dish and spoon in the filling. Pour the tomato sauce over and around the shells and bake in the oven for 25–30 minutes.

Serve as a starter or as a main course.

ACCOMPANIMENT DISHES

Dieters' ratatouille

See pages 24–5

Serves 4

Each serving: 40 kcal/170 kJ, 10 g (1 unit) carbohydrate, 4 g fibre, 2 g protein, negligible fat

1 medium-sized onion, sliced
1 aubergine, sliced
1 medium-sized green pepper, sliced into rings
1 medium-sized red pepper, sliced into rings
2 courgettes or small marrows, sliced
1 tsp garlic salt
pepper
pinch thyme
300 g/10½ oz canned tomatoes, chopped with juice

Heat the oven to 190°C/375°F/gas 5.

Place the onion, aubergine, peppers and courgettes in a non-stick ovenproof casserole. Add the garlic salt, pepper and thyme to the tomato liquid and mix well. Pour the tomatoes and liquid over the vegetables in the casserole and cook in the oven for 30–45 minutes or until the vegetables are tender but not soft.

Try making this ratatouille with other vegetables. Serve hot or cold.

Crisp vegetable fry

Serves 4

Each serving: 70 kcal/290 kJ, 10 g (1 unit) carbohydrate, 7 g fibre, 3 g protein, 2 g fat

½ tbsp sunflower or other polyunsaturated oil
200 g/7 oz French beans, thinly sliced
4 spring onions, finely chopped
200 g/7 oz canned sweetcorn kernels
1 medium-sized red pepper, chopped
200 g/7 oz fresh or canned bean sprouts
2 tsp soya sauce
2 tsp lemon juice
1 tsp chopped capers (optional)
1 tsp chopped gherkins (optional)
seasoning

Heat the oil in a non-stick pan. Add all the vegetables and fry gently for 6–8 minutes, stirring occasionally. Add the soya sauce, lemon juice, capers and pickles, if using, and cook for a further 3–5 minutes. Add seasoning and serve as part of a Chinese meal, or as an accompaniment to a snack.

Chinese bean sprouts and radishes

Serves 4

Each serving: 50 kcal/210 kJ, negligible (0 units) carbohydrate, 2 g fibre, 1 g protein, 4 g fat

1 tbsp polyunsaturated oil
60 g/2 oz radishes, thinly sliced
225 g/8 oz bean sprouts
6 spring onions, thinly sliced
2 tbsp dry sherry
1 tsp soya sauce, or to taste
seasoning

Heat the oil in a non-stick pan. Add the radishes and cook for 1 minute, stirring. Add the bean sprouts and the spring onions and continue to cook for 1 minute. Add the sherry and soya sauce and cook for 3 minutes, stirring. Season and serve as part of a Chinese meal.

PULSES

Bacon beanpot

Serves 4

Each serving: 290 kcal/1220 kJ, 30 g (3 units) carbohydrate, 15 g fibre, 25 g protein, 9 g fat

1 tbsp polyunsaturated oil
2 medium-sized onions, sliced
1 clove garlic, crushed
100 g/3½ oz black-eyed beans, soaked (see pages 12–13)
100 g/3½ oz lima beans, soaked (see pages 12–13)
850 ml/1½ pt stock
1 tbsp tomato purée
¼–½ tsp tabasco sauce
1 bay leaf
200 g/7 oz boiled lean bacon, diced
200 g/7 oz French beans, cut into 25 mm/1 in lengths
seasoning
1 tbsp wholemeal flour

Heat the oil in a large flameproof casserole. Add the onions and fry gently for 5 minutes. Add the garlic, drained beans, stock, tomato purée, tabasco sauce and bay leaf. Bring to the boil and boil gently for 10 minutes. Reduce the heat and simmer for 1 hour, or until the beans are tender. Add the bacon, French beans and seasoning and simmer for a further 15 minutes. Remove the bay leaf.

Blend the flour with a little water, stir into the casserole and return to the boil. Simmer for a further 3 minutes or until thickened, then serve.

Brazilian beans with Continental sausage

Serves 4

Each serving: 270 kcal/1130 kJ, 30 g (3 units) carbohydrate, 17 g fibre, 18 g protein, 8 g fat

200 g/7 oz black-eyed, or other, beans, soaked (see page 12)
1 tbsp polyunsaturated oil
250 ml/9 fl oz stock
2 medium-sized leeks, thinly sliced
1 clove garlic, crushed
2 rashers lean bacon, chopped
4 medium-sized tomatoes, chopped
60 g/2 oz Continental or beef sausage, grilled and diced
1–2 tsp chilli powder, or to taste
seasoning
2 tbsp chopped parsley

Cook the beans (see page 13).

Meanwhile, heat the oil with a few spoonfuls of stock in a flameproof casserole and gently cook the leeks, garlic and bacon for 10 minutes, stirring occasionally. Add the beans and the remaining ingredients, bring to the boil and simmer for 25–30 minutes. Adjust the seasoning before serving if necessary. In Brazil, this dish is usually highly seasoned.

Serve accompanied by a mound of Brown Rice with Orange (see page 40).

Bean and tomato loaf

Serves 4

Each serving: 180 kcal/760 kJ, 30 g (3 units) carbohydrate, 9 g fibre, 10 g protein, 4 g fat

115 g/4 oz butter beans, soaked (see page 12)
1 medium-sized onion, chopped
1 small bay leaf
120 ml/4 fl oz Tomato Sauce (see pages 100–1)
1 egg, beaten
60 g/2 oz Weetabix, crushed
1 small green chilli, finely chopped
seasoning

Heat the oven to 190°C/375°F/gas 5.

Cook the beans with the onion and bay leaf in about a ½ litre/18 fl oz water (see page 13). Drain off any excess liquid and mash with a fork. Add all the remaining ingredients and mix well.

Put the mixture into a 450 g/1 lb non-stick loaf tin or other suitable baking dish, and bake for 45–50 minutes, or until firm. Turn out of the dish and cut into slices. Serve hot with vegetables or cold with salad.

Beans and mushrooms

Serves 4

Each serving: 200 kcal/840 kJ, 30 g (3 units) carbohydrate, 16 g fibre, 12 g protein, 5 g fat

1 tbsp polyunsaturated margarine
2–3 tbsp stock
1 large onion, finely chopped
300 g/10½ oz mushrooms, sliced
600 g/21 oz baked beans
1 tsp soya sauce
1 tbsp Worcester sauce
seasoning
pinch dried marjoram
4 tbsp chopped parsley
4 thin-cut slices wholemeal bread from a small loaf, toasted
1 tsp paprika

Melt the margarine with the stock and fry the onion and mushrooms until the onion starts to brown. Add the beans, sauces, seasoning and marjoram and simmer until heated through. Serve sprinkled with parsley on a hot dish. Cut the toast into triangles and arrange as a border around the bean and mushroom mixture. Sprinkle the toast with paprika before serving.

Lentils with tomatoes

Serves 4

Each serving: 470 kcal/1970 kJ, 80 g (8 units) carbohydrate, 13 g fibre, 23 g protein, 5 g fat

300 g/10½ oz brown lentils
1 tbsp corn oil
1 large onion, chopped
2 cloves garlic, crushed
1 tsp ground cumin
6 tbsp beef stock
4 medium-sized tomatoes, chopped
seasoning
200 g/7 oz long-grain brown rice
15 g/½ oz grated Parmesan cheese

Boil the lentils for 10 minutes then simmer for 20 minutes. Drain.

Heat the oil in a large saucepan. Add the onion and garlic and fry gently for 5 minutes until transparent. Stir in the cumin and cook over high heat for 2 minutes. Add the stock and lentils and simmer gently, uncovered, for about 15 minutes, or until the lentils are nearly tender. Stir in the tomatoes and seasoning and simmer for 10–15 minutes or until the tomatoes are tender.

Meanwhile, cook the rice (see page 14). Pour the lentil mixture into the centre of a hot serving dish and spoon a border of rice around it. Sprinkle the Parmesan cheese over the top before serving.

Casserole of chick peas with vegetables

Serves 4

Each serving: 320 kcal/1340 kJ, 50 g (5 units) carbohydrate, 16 g fibre, 18 g protein, 8 g fat

300 g/10½ oz chick peas, soaked (see page 12)
1 tbsp corn oil
1 medium-sized onion, chopped
1 clove garlic, crushed
450 g/1 lb tomatoes, chopped
½ small cabbage, finely shredded
1 medium-sized green pepper, sliced
1 medium-sized carrot, diced or coarsely grated
½ tsp ground cumin
½ tsp ground ginger
pinch ground cloves
seasoning
300 ml/½ pt strong stock
4 tbsp chopped parsley

Cook the peas until nearly tender (see page 13). Drain and set aside. Heat the oil in a saucepan. Add the onion and garlic and fry gently for 5 minutes until transparent. Add the remaining vegetables, cover and cook over gentle heat for 10 minutes, stirring occasionally. Stir in the spices, seasoning, stock and drained peas. Re-cover, then simmer for 15–20 minutes or until the vegetables are tender but not soft. Stir in half the parsley and sprinkle the remainder on top before serving.

Vegetarian two-bean savoury

Serves 4

Each serving: 140 kcal/590 kJ, 20 g (2 units) carbohydrate, 13 g fibre, 10 g protein, 5 g fat

1 tbsp polyunsaturated oil
2 large onions, chopped
400 g/14 oz canned broad beans
4 tbsp chopped parsley
1–2 small sprigs of marjoram
*150 ml/¼ pt vegetable stock**
seasoning
100 g/3½ oz garden peas
400 g/14 oz French beans, in short lengths
1 clove garlic, crushed
150 ml/¼ pt low-fat plain yoghurt
paprika

Heat oil in a saucepan. Add the onions and fry gently for 5 minutes until golden brown. Add the broad beans, parsley and marjoram and cook gently for 5 minutes, turning frequently. Add the stock, seasoning, peas and French beans, cover and cook until all are almost tender. Remove the lid for the remainder of cooking (5–10 minutes) to allow excess liquid to evaporate. Mix the garlic into the yoghurt, stir into the vegetables and return to the heat for 2 minutes. Sprinkle with paprika before serving.

Tuscan beans with pasta

See pages 24–5

Serves 4

Each serving: 410 kcal/1720 kJ, 60 g (6 units) carbohydrate, 24 g fibre, 21 g protein, 10 g fat

300 g/10½ oz haricot beans, soaked (see page 12)
2 tbsp polyunsaturated oil
1–2 cloves garlic, crushed
2 tbsp chopped parsley
2 fresh sage leaves
200 g/7 oz canned plum tomatoes, chopped with juice
1 tbsp tomato purée
2 medium-sized red peppers, chopped
seasoning
400 g/14 oz cooked wholemeal pasta, in novelty shapes
2 tbsp chopped parsley

Cook the beans (see page 13). Heat the oil in a saucepan. Add the hot beans, garlic, parsley and sage and cook gently for 5 minutes.

Meanwhile, mash together the tomatoes and tomato purée and stir them into the beans along with the red peppers and seasoning. Return to the boil and simmer for 30 minutes. Spoon the bean

---

*Non-vegetarians may prefer to use chicken stock.

mixture into the centre of a serving dish and arrange the pasta around the outside. Sprinkle the pasta with parsley before serving.

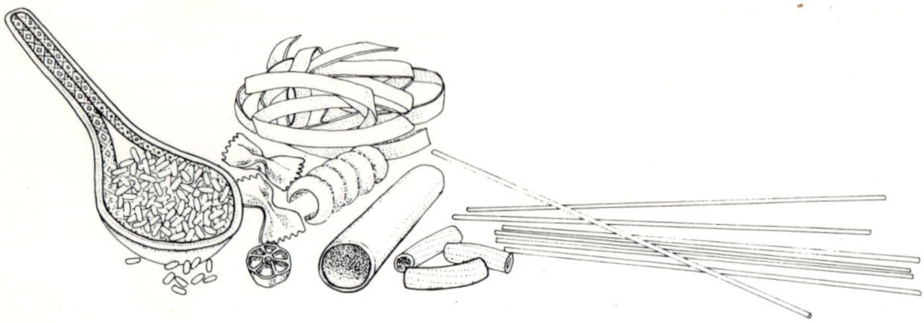

RICE AND PASTA

RICE DISHES

Spanish rice

See pages 24–5

Serves 4

Each serving: 280 kcal/1180 kJ, 40 g (4 units) carbohydrate, 14 g fibre, 13 g protein, 8 g fat

1 tbsp polyunsaturated oil
2 tbsp stock
1 large Spanish onion, finely chopped
1 clove garlic, crushed
4 large tomatoes, chopped
4 tbsp chopped parsley
1 tsp chopped marjoram or ½ tsp dried marjoram
seasoning
250 g/9 oz cooked long-grain brown rice (see page 14)
400 g/14 oz red kidney beans canned without sugar or cooked beans (see pages 12–13).
12 black olives, halved and stoned
1 hard-boiled egg, chopped
2 tbsp chopped parsley

Heat the oil with the stock and fry the onion and garlic gently for 5 minutes until transparent. Add the tomatoes, herbs and seasoning, cover and cook over medium heat until the ingredients are heated through, shaking the pan occasionally. Add the rice and beans and heat through.

Turn out on to a hot serving dish and garnish with olives, egg and parsley before serving.

Indonesian rice

Serves 4
Each serving: 280 kcal/1180 kJ, 40 g (4 units) carbohydrate, 4 g fibre, 18 g protein, 5 g fat

200 g/7 oz long-grain brown rice
2 shallots or small onions, finely chopped
1 clove garlic, crushed
1 tsp ground coriander
½ tsp ground cumin
¼ tsp chilli powder
1 tsp salt (omit if stock cube is used)
pepper
540 ml/18 fl oz chicken stock
100 g/3½ oz canned shrimps, drained
100 g/3½ oz cooked chicken meat, chopped
1 egg, beaten

Heat the oven to 180°C/350°F/gas 4.

Place the rice, shallots, garlic, spices and seasoning in an ovenproof dish and add the stock. Cover and cook in the oven for 1 hour. Stir in the shrimps and chicken and return to the oven for 15 minutes. Fry the beaten egg in a non-stick pan, then shred into noodle-like strips. Remove the rice from the oven, fluff up with a fork (it should be dry and flaky), sprinkle strips of egg on top and serve.

Rice with chicken and mushrooms

Serves 4
Each serving: 400 kcal/1680 kJ, 50 g (5 units) carbohydrate, 9 g fibre, 23 g protein, 7 g fat

200 g/7 oz uncooked chicken (white meat), diced
seasoning
450 ml/¾ pt chicken stock
250 ml/9 fl oz dry white wine or cider (or use extra stock)
bouquet garni (parsley, bay leaf and tarragon)
1 tbsp polyunsaturated oil
1 medium-sized onion, chopped
60 g/2 oz lean cooked ham, cut into thin strips
1 tbsp brandy (optional)
200 g/7 oz long-grain brown rice
pinch each dried marjoram, thyme and basil
300 g/10½ oz fresh or frozen peas
100 g/3½ oz flat mushrooms, grilled and chopped
1 tbsp grated Parmesan cheese

Season the chicken and place in a small saucepan with 150 ml/¼ pt of stock and 150 ml/¼ pt wine or cider. Add the bouquet garni, bring to the boil and simmer, covered, for 30–40 minutes or until tender. Heat the oil in a flameproof casserole, add the onion and fry gently until it starts to brown. Add the chicken mixture and ham and cook for about 3 minutes, stirring occasionally. Add the remaining wine and the brandy, if using, and bring to the boil. Sprinkle in the rice and simmer gently until the stock is absorbed. Add the remaining stock, herbs and seasoning and simmer gently for about 20 minutes, then stir in the peas and continue to cook until the rice is tender. A few minutes before serving sprinkle over the mushrooms and cheese. Serve straight from the casserole.

Brown rice with orange

Serves 4
Each serving: 130 kcal/550 kJ, 30 g (3 units) carbohydrate, 3 g fibre, 3 g protein, negligible fat

500 g/18 oz cooked long-grain brown rice (see page 14)
1 large orange, sectioned and chopped
rind of 1 orange, cut into matchsticks
1 tbsp chopped tarragon
*1 tbsp chopped chervil (optional)**
2 tbsp bottled oil-free French dressing

While the rice is cooking, scrub the orange, remove the orange part of the rind and cut into fine strips. Soak in boiling water for 10 minutes. (Alternatively, grate the rind). Mix all the ingredients together and serve hot or cold as an accompaniment to a main dish.

PASTA DISHES

Cocido Andaluz

Serves 4
Each serving: 370 kcal/1550 kJ, 60 g (6 units) carbohydrate, 13 g fibre, 20 g protein, 7 g fat

1 tbsp polyunsaturated oil
1 medium-sized onion, chopped
1 medium-sized leek, chopped
2 rashers lean bacon, chopped
300 g/10½ oz canned tomatoes, chopped with juice
150 ml/¼ pt stock
2 tbsp tomato purée
2 tsp vinegar
1 medium-sized carrot, chopped
1 medium-sized green pepper, chopped
150 g/5 oz cooked haricot, or other, beans (see pages 12–13)
1 clove garlic, crushed
60 g/2 oz Continental or chipolata sausage, grilled and chopped until the size of breadcrumbs
seasoning
250 g/9 oz wholemeal spaghetti

Heat the oil in a saucepan. Add the onion and leek and fry gently for 5 minutes until transparent. Add the bacon and cook until lightly browned. Add the tomatoes, stock, tomato purée and vinegar, bring to the boil and simmer for 10 minutes. Add the carrot, green pepper, beans, garlic, sausage and seasoning and simmer for a further 20 minutes.

---

*Other seasonings may be substituted, depending on the dish it is to accompany – for example soya sauce, or coriander or lemon juice if the rice is to accompany a Chinese or Indian dish.

Meanwhile, cook the spaghetti in boiling salted water (see page 15). Drain and turn out on to a hot serving dish. Pour over the meat mixture and serve.

Lasagne Florentine

Serves 4
Each serving: 280 kcal/1180 kJ, 30 g (3 units) carbohydrate, 11 g fibre, 24 g protein, 8 g fat

125 g/4½ oz wholemeal lasagne
1 kg/2¼ lb spinach or 500 g pack frozen spinach

Sauce
300 ml/½ pt low-fat plain yoghurt
100 g/3½ oz skimmed milk curd cheese or sieved cottage cheese
2 eggs
pinch grated nutmeg
seasoning
3 tbsp grated Parmesan cheese
3 tbsp wholemeal breadcrumbs
paprika

Heat the oven to 190°C/375°F/gas 5.

Cook the lasagne in boiling salted water until half-cooked and drain carefully (see page 15). Meanwhile, cook the spinach until it is just tender, drain well and chop roughly.

To make the sauce, beat the yoghurt, cheese, eggs, nutmeg and seasoning together. Place a layer of spinach in a deep non-stick baking dish, then top with a layer of lasagne and sauce. Repeat these layers, finishing with the remaining sauce. Mix the Parmesan cheese and breadcrumbs together, sprinkle on top and bake in the oven for 25–30 minutes. Sprinkle a little paprika on top before serving.

Pasta spirals with mushrooms, ham and tomato

Serves 4
Each serving: 400 kcal/1680 kJ, 60 g (6 units) carbohydrate, 11 g fibre, 16 g protein, 10 g fat

300 g/10½ oz wholemeal pasta spirals or spaghetti
225 g/8 oz mushrooms, sliced
1 tbsp polyunsaturated oil
1 clove garlic, crushed
2 medium-sized tomatoes, chopped
100 g/3½ oz lean ham, chopped
100 g/3½ oz canned or cooked sweetcorn kernels
1 tsp chopped basil or to taste
2 tbsp chopped parsley
pepper
1 egg, beaten
2 tbsp grated Parmesan cheese

Cook the pasta in boiling salted water (see page 15). Drain.

Meanwhile, cook the mushrooms gently in the oil, add the garlic and tomatoes and cook for a further 5 minutes. Stir in the ham,

corn, herbs and pepper and heat through, stirring occasionally.
Put the cooked pasta into a heated dish and keep hot. Withdraw the vegetable saucepan quickly from the heat and stir in the beaten egg immediately. Just when the mixture starts to thicken (it should be the consistency of fairly thick cream), quickly pour it over the pasta. Sprinkle with the cheese and stir the whole mixture to distribute the sauce and coat the pasta. Serve immediately.

Pasta with piquant fish sauce

Serves 4
Each serving: 340 kcal/1430 kJ, 50 g (5 units) carbohydrate, 9 g fibre, 17 g protein, 7 g fat

1 tbsp polyunsaturated oil
1 small onion, chopped
1 clove garlic, crushed
300 g/10½ oz canned tomatoes, chopped with juice
200 g/7 oz canned tuna fish in brine, drained and flaked
2 tbsp capers, roughly chopped
3 tsp anchovy essence
1 tbsp finely grated orange rind
seasoning
2 tbsp chopped parsley
300 g/10½ oz wholemeal spaghetti

Heat the oil in a large saucepan. Add the onion and garlic and fry gently for about 10 minutes, stirring occasionally. Stir in the tomatoes and simmer for a further 15 minutes. Add the tuna, capers, anchovy essence, orange rind and seasoning and bring to the simmer. Cook for 10 minutes, then stir in the parsley.
Meanwhile, cook the spaghetti in boiling salted water (see page 15). Drain well, place in a hot serving dish and pour over the sauce.

Macaroni bake

Serves 4
Each serving: 370 kcal/1550 kJ, 50 g (5 units) carbohydrate, 10 g fibre, 24 g protein, 8 g fat

1 tbsp polyunsaturated margarine
4½ tbsp wholemeal flour
450 ml/¾ pt skimmed milk
salt and pepper
1 tsp dry mustard
100 g/3½ oz skimmed milk curd cheese or cottage cheese
150 g/5 oz short-cut wholemeal macaroni, cooked (see page 15)
100 g/3½ oz mushrooms, sliced
200 g/7 oz canned sweetcorn kernels
4 tbsp chopped mixed peppers
150 g/5 oz canned tuna fish in brine, drained and flaked
6 tbsp wholemeal breadcrumbs
2 tbsp grated Parmesan cheese

Heat the oven to 200°C/400°F/gas 6.
Melt the margarine in a saucepan. Remove from the heat and stir in the flour until smooth. Gradually add the skimmed milk then return to the heat and simmer for 2–3 minutes, stirring until

thickened. Stir in the seasoning, mustard and cheese and simmer for a further 2 minutes.

Mix together the macaroni, mushrooms, corn, peppers and tuna and toss in the cheese sauce. Pour the mixture into a non-stick ovenproof dish. Mix the breadcrumbs and Parmesan cheese and sprinkle over the top. Bake for 15–20 minutes and serve as a snack, supper dish or with vegetables as a main dish.

FISH, POULTRY AND MEAT

FISH DISHES

Quick fish pie

Serves 4

Each serving: 300 kcal/1260 kJ, 40 g (4 units) carbohydrate, 9 g fibre, 18 g protein, 8 g fat

300 ml/½ pt canned mushroom soup (reconstituted volume if condensed)
200 g/7 oz poached white fish, flaked
1 hard-boiled egg, chopped
300 g/10½ oz fresh or frozen sweetcorn kernels, cooked
*300 g/10½ oz canned or frozen mixed vegetables**
3 medium-sized cooked potatoes, thinly sliced
½ tsp garlic salt
2 tbsp skimmed milk

Mix the soup, fish, egg, corn and mixed vegetables together in a saucepan and simmer gently for 15 minutes to heat through thoroughly. Transfer to a non-stick pie dish. Arrange the potatoes in overlapping slices on top. Mix the garlic salt with the milk and brush over the potatoes, brown under a medium grill and serve hot.

Alternatively, the pie can be prepared in advance, cooled and kept in the refrigerator then cooked at 190°C/375°F/gas 5 for 25–30 minutes.

---

*Calculated as equal amounts of carrots, peas, green beans and turnip.

Salmon flan

Serves 4

Each serving: 300 kcal/1260 kJ, 30 g (3 units) carbohydrate, 8 g fibre, 18 g protein, 13 g fat

20 cm/8 in flan case, baked blind (see page 90)
150 g/5 oz canned salmon
100 g/3½ oz canned mushrooms, sliced
1 tbsp polyunsaturated margarine
1 tbsp finely chopped onion
1 stalk celery, finely chopped
1 small green pepper, chopped
1½ tbsp wholemeal flour
¼ tsp garlic salt
100 ml/3½ fl oz skimmed milk
3 tsp anchovy essence
150 g/5 oz cooked mung beans (see pages 12–13)
1 small red pepper, sliced into rings

While the flan case is baking, drain the salmon and mushrooms and reserve the liquid from the cans. Melt the margarine in a non-stick pan. Add the onion, celery and green pepper and cook until tender, stirring occasionally. Stir in the flour and salt.

Mix the salmon and mushroom liquids with the milk and add to the pan, stirring until the liquid comes to the boil. Boil for 3 minutes. Add the anchovy essence, salmon, mushrooms and beans to the pan and heat thoroughly. Pour into the pastry case. Serve hot or cold, garnished with the sliced red pepper.

Canned tuna or pilchards may be substituted for the salmon.

Baked fish with mushrooms

Serves 4

Each serving: 150 kcal/620 kJ, negligible (0 units) carbohydrate, 2 g fibre, 20 g protein, 6 g fat

400 g/14 oz white fish fillets, skinned (4 fillets)
150 ml/¼pt skimmed milk
5 tbsp dry white wine
4 tbsp finely chopped parsley, stalks reserved
30 g/1 oz polyunsaturated margarine
225 g/8 oz mushrooms, sliced
onion salt
pepper
2 tsp lemon juice
pinch grated nutmeg
lemon wedges

Heat the oven to 180°C/350°F/gas 4.

Simmer the fish trimmings, milk, wine, parsley stalks and 3 tbsp water together for 20 minutes.

Meanwhile, melt the margarine in a saucepan. Add the mushrooms and stir to absorb the fat for 1–2 minutes over low heat. Stir in half the chopped parsley, the seasoning and lemon juice. Remove from the heat. Place the fish fillets, side by side, in a fairly shallow non-stick ovenproof dish. Strain the milk mixture and pour over the fish. Sprinkle on the nutmeg, spoon over the mushroom mixture and cover with a lid or foil. Bake for 20–25 minutes, or until the fish is cooked. Sprinkle liberally with the remaining parsley and garnish with the lemon wedges before serving.

POULTRY DISHES

Sweet and sour chicken

Serves 4

Each serving: 340 kcal/1430 kJ, 40 g (4 units) carbohydrate, 13 g fibre, 26 g protein, 9 g fat

1 tbsp polyunsaturated oil
150 ml/¼ pt chicken stock
1 medium-sized onion, sliced
1 clove garlic, crushed
200 g/7 oz cooked chicken, diced
300 g/10½ oz cooked mung beans (see pages 12–13)
200 g/7 oz carrots, cut into matchstick pieces
1 medium-sized red pepper, sliced
1 medium-sized green pepper, sliced
*100 g/3½ oz skinned cooked chestnuts, chopped**
4 pineapple rings, canned without sugar, diced
8 tbsp natural juice from canned pineapple
3 tbsp wholemeal flour
3 tsp soya sauce
3 tbsp vinegar
seasoning

Heat the oil with a few spoonfuls of stock and cook the onion and garlic gently for about 5 minutes. Add the chicken, mung beans, carrots, peppers and chestnuts and cook gently for 5 minutes, stirring occasionally. Add the remainder of the stock and simmer for 15–20 minutes. Add the pineapple and bring to the boil.

Blend the flour with the remaining ingredients, stir into the mixture and cook for 3 minutes to thicken. Adjust the seasoning and serve.

Chicken casserole with mixed vegetables

Serves 4

Each serving: 270 kcal/1130 kJ, 20 g (2 units) carbohydrate, 8 g fibre, 24 g protein, 9 g fat

1 tbsp polyunsaturated oil
400 ml/14 fl oz chicken stock
340 g/12 oz chicken, cut into neat pieces
2 medium-sized onions, finely chopped
seasoning
2 stalks celery, chopped
2 medium-sized leeks, sliced
100 g/3½ oz runner beans, chopped
200 g/7 oz sweetcorn kernels
2 tbsp wholemeal flour

---

*Reconstituted dried chestnuts can be used.

Heat the oven to 190°C/375°F/gas 5.

Heat the oil with a few spoonfuls of stock in a large flameproof casserole and fry the chicken pieces until they are pale golden brown. Remove from the pan and add the onions. Cook gently for 5 minutes, stirring occasionally. Add the remaining stock, chicken and seasoning and bring to the boil. Cover and cook in the oven for 20 minutes. Add the remaining vegetables and cook for a further 30 minutes or until all the vegetables are cooked.

Blend the flour with a little cold water, stir into the mixture and cook for 5 minutes until thickened. Adjust the seasoning and serve.

Mexican chicken

Serves 4

Each serving: 290 kcal/1220 kJ, 20 g (2 units) carbohydrate, 8 g fibre, 32 g protein, 8 g fat

340 g/12 oz cooked chicken, cut into neat pieces
200 ml/⅓ pt low-fat plain yoghurt
1–3 tsp chilli powder, or to taste
1 tbsp paprika
onion salt
¼–½ tsp prepared mustard
2 medium-sized red peppers, finely diced
400 g/14 oz canned corn kernels
225 g/8 oz button mushrooms
1 bunch spring onions, white and green, chopped

Put the chicken pieces into a shallow dish. Mix the yoghurt, chilli powder, paprika, salt and mustard together and pour over the chicken. Stir to coat the chicken well and leave to marinate for 1–2 hours at room temperature. Add the peppers to the chicken mixture and transfer to a non-stick saucepan. Cook the mixture over medium heat for about 15 minutes, stirring frequently. Add some liquid from the can of corn kernels or a little stock if the mixture becomes too thick.

Meanwhile, heat the corn kernels until hot and poach the mushrooms in water until tender. Drain. Spoon the chicken into the centre of a hot serving dish and sprinkle on the spring onions. Arrange the corn, interspaced with mushrooms, around the outside. Serve with plainly cooked brown rice (see page 14).

Pancakes* stuffed with turkey

Serves 4 (makes 8 pancakes)

Each serving: 280 kcal/1180 kJ, 30 g (3 units) carbohydrate, 6 g fibre, 18 g protein, 9 g fat

Basic Pancake recipe (see page 75)
Wine and Mushroom Sauce (½ quantity of recipe on page 100)

Filling
1 tbsp polyunsaturated oil
1 medium-sized onion, chopped
100 g/3½ oz cooked turkey, minced
100 g/3½ oz cooked haricot, or other beans (see pages 12–13) mashed with the turkey
3 tbsp chopped parsley or other herbs
seasoning

Heat the oven to 200°C/400°F/gas 6.

Make the pancakes and stack until required.

To make the filling, heat the oil in a pan. Add the onion and fry gently until golden brown, then add the remaining filling ingredients and 3 tbsp of the Wine and Mushroom Sauce. Divide the mixture between the pancakes, roll up each one like a cigar and place in a shallow, non-stick baking dish. Cover with the remainder of the wine and mushroom sauce and bake for 15–20 minutes or until heated through. Serve with freshly cooked vegetables.

MEAT DISHES

Veal and ham with beans

Serves 4
Each serving: 260 kcal/1090 kJ, 20 g (2 units) carbohydrate, 7 g fibre, 24 g protein, 8 g fat

15 g/½ oz polyunsaturated margarine
300 ml/½ pt skimmed milk
6 tbsp white meat stock
3 tbsp wholemeal flour
2 medium-sized red peppers, chopped (or use canned)
150 g/5 oz cooked veal, cubed
60 g/2 oz cooked ham, diced
300 g/10½ oz cooked haricot beans (see pages 12–13)
2 tbsp chopped capers
seasoning
1 tbsp lemon juice
2 tbsp chopped parsley

Add the margarine to the milk and stock and bring to the boil. Blend the flour with a little reserved liquid and stir into the mixture. Return to the boil and simmer for about 3 minutes. Stir in the peppers, veal, ham, beans and capers, season and heat through for about 10 minutes. Just before serving, stir in the lemon juice and parsley.

Serve with a border of mashed potatoes, and accompanied by other vegetables.

---

*Wholemeal dinner pancakes (crêpes) can be bought at some delicatessens. Filled, these can turn left-over scraps of meat, beans and brown rice (or dishes made with these ingredients) into interesting family meals, or meals for entertaining. Pouring a sauce over is optional. Everything could be assembled when hot, using a bought low-calorie bottled sauce in the filling instead of the home-made sauces on pages 98–101.

Veal in red wine

Serves 4

Each serving: 400 kcal/1680 kJ, 50 g (5 units) carbohydrate, 24 g fibre, 35 g protein, 7 g fat

1 tbsp polyunsaturated oil
600 ml/1 pt chicken or other white stock
300 g/10½ oz pie veal, cubed
2 medium-sized onions, chopped
3 medium-sized carrots, thinly sliced
2 stalks celery, chopped
1 clove garlic, crushed
3 tbsp wholemeal flour
150 ml/¼ pt dry red wine
bouquet garni (rosemary, parsley and bay leaf)
*300 g/10½ oz aduki beans, soaked (see page 12)**
seasoning
2 tbsp chopped parsley
2 tsp finely chopped lemon rind

Heat the oil with a few spoonfuls of stock in a flameproof casserole and fry the meat until golden brown. Remove from the casserole with a slotted spoon. Add the onions to the pan and fry gently until pale brown. Stir in the carrots, celery and garlic and cook slowly, covered, for about 10 minutes. Sprinkle in the flour and cook for a few minutes, stirring. Add the wine, the remaining stock, bouquet garni and beans. Cover and cook slowly for 1½ hours. Stir in the seasoning and continue to cook for about 10 minutes, or until all ingredients are tender. Just before serving remove the bouquet garni and garnish with chopped lemon rind and parsley.

Mexican beef paprika

Serves 4

Each serving: 160 kcal/670 kJ, 20 g (2 units) carbohydrate, 7 g fibre, 17 g protein, 3 g fat

200 g/7 oz lean stewing steak, diced
2 tbsp paprika
1 large red pepper, sliced (or use canned)
2 large Spanish onions, sliced
4 stalks celery, sliced
200 g/7 oz butter beans canned without sugar, or cooked beans (see pages 12–13)
seasoning
300 g/10½ oz canned tomatoes, drained
300–450 ml/½–¾ pt stock

Heat the oven to 170°C/325°F/gas 3.

Toss the meat in the paprika, then place in layers, with the vegetables, in an ovenproof casserole. Season the layers with salt and lightly with pepper. Add the stock, cover with a tight-fitting

---

*After soaking, the beans should be boiled rapidly for 10 minutes before being added to the casserole.

lid and cook in the oven for 1½–2 hours or until all the ingredients are tender.

Serve straight from the casserole. Jacket potatoes could be cooked in the oven at the same time.

Steak and kidney hot-pot

Serves 4

Each serving: 170 kcal/710 kJ, 20 g (2 units) carbohydrate, 9 g fibre, 17 g protein, 2 g fat

100 g/3½ oz lean stewing steak, diced
100 g/3½ oz lamb's kidney, skinned, cored and diced
1 large onion, thinly sliced
2 medium-sized carrots, sliced
4 stalks celery, sliced
1 tsp meat extract
2 tsp Worcester sauce
seasoning
3 tbsp wholemeal flour
200 g/7 oz red kidney beans canned without sugar, or cooked beans (see pages 12–13)
2 young leeks, thinly sliced

Place the steak, kidney, onion, carrots and celery in layers in a flameproof casserole. Dissolve the meat extract in hot water, top up with cold water and add enough, along with the Worcester sauce, to come level with the top of the vegetables in the casserole. Season lightly. Simmer gently for 1 hour. Blend the flour with a little cold water and mix into the casserole. Bring back to the boil and cook gently for about 3 minutes. Stir in the beans and leeks and continue cooking for about 30 minutes. Adjust the seasoning and serve straight from the casserole.

Jamaican beef and bean casserole

Serves 4

Each serving: 280 kcal/1180 kJ, 20 g (2 units) carbohydrate, 8 g fibre, 25 g protein, 12 g fat

1 tbsp polyunsaturated oil
250 ml/9 fl oz beef stock
2 medium-sized onions, sliced
225 g/8 oz lean stewing steak, diced
2 tbsp wholemeal flour
2 green chillies, seeded and finely chopped
1 clove garlic, chopped
½ tsp ground ginger, or to taste
400 g/14 oz canned tomatoes, chopped with juice
½ tsp dried thyme or oregano
seasoning
400 g/14 oz cooked soya beans (see pages 12–13)
200 g/7 oz mixed peppers, diced
2 tbsp chopped chives

Heat the oil with a few spoonfuls of stock in a large saucepan and fry the onions gently until golden brown. Toss the meat in the flour and add to the saucepan. Cook for 10 minutes, stirring occasionally. Add the chillies, garlic and ginger and simmer slowly for 5 minutes. Stir in the tomatoes, thyme, and the remaining stock, and season. Bring to the boil, cover, and simmer slowly for 1 hour. Add the beans and simmer for a further 30–45 minutes or until the meat is very tender and the beans have absorbed the flavours of the meat and have started to break down. Adjust the seasoning if necessary.

Stir in half the peppers, scattering the remainder evenly over the top. Cover and simmer gently for 5 minutes. Sprinkle the chives on top and serve straight from the casserole, accompanied by potatoes boiled in their skins.

Cape bredie

Serves 4

Each serving: 330 kcal/1390 kJ, 40 g (4 units) carbohydrate, 17 g fibre, 25 g protein, 9 g fat

1 tbsp polyunsaturated oil
2 large onions, thinly sliced
680 g/1½ lb tomatoes, sliced
1–2 chillies, seeded and finely chopped
2 cloves
1 clove garlic, crushed
25 mm/1 in piece root ginger, finely chopped
seasoning
pinch cayenne pepper
200 g/7 oz lean lamb, diced
200 g/7 oz black-eyed beans, soaked (see page 12)
400 ml/ 14 fl oz meat stock
2 tbsp wholemeal flour

Heat the oil with a few spoonfuls of water in a flameproof casserole. Stir in the onions, cover with a tight-fitting lid and cook over low heat for about 20 minutes, stirring occasionally. Arrange the tomatoes in a layer over the onions, then sprinkle over the chillies, cloves, garlic, root ginger, seasoning and cayenne. Add the meat and beans and enough stock to come level with the top of the ingredients. Bring to the boil and boil gently for 10 minutes. Re-cover and simmer gently for 45–60 minutes or until the meat and beans are tender.

Blend the flour with a little water, stir in to the casserole and return to the boil. Cook for a further 5 minutes or until thickened. Serve with plainly cooked brown rice (see page 14).

Chop Suey (top, see p. 58), Chinese-style Rice (bottom right, see p. 59), Sweet and Sour Sauce (bottom left, see p. 100).

Italian lamb casserole

Serves 4

Each serving: 430 kcal/1810 kJ, 60 g (6 units) carbohydrate, 19 g fibre, 28 g protein, 10 g fat

1 tbsp polyunsaturated oil
2 medium-sized onions, thinly sliced
225 g/8 oz lean lamb, diced
200 g/7 oz barlotti or haricot beans, soaked (see page 12)
1 tbsp tomato purée
450 g/16 oz canned tomatoes, chopped with the juice
3 medium-sized peppers, sliced
1 tsp dried oregano or 1 tbsp chopped oregano
450–600 ml/¾–1 pt stock
600 g/1 lb 5 oz potatoes, diced
garlic salt
pepper
5 tbsp chopped parsley

Heat the oil in a large saucepan. Add the onions and fry gently until transparent. Add the lamb and cook for a further 10 minutes, stirring occasionally. Stir in the beans, tomato purée, tomatoes, peppers, oregano and stock. Cover and boil gently for 10 minutes. Sprinkle over the potatoes in a thick layer, cover and simmer for 1–1½ hours. Ten minutes before serving, stir in the garlic salt and pepper, disturbing the potatoes as little as possible. Sprinkle a little salt over the potatoes, brown under a medium grill and scatter parsley over the top before serving.

Alternatively, cook in the oven at 140–190°C/275–375°F/gas 2–5. Remove the lid about 30 minutes before serving to let the potatoes become brown and crisp.

Spanish pork with courgettes

Serves 4

Each serving: 280 kcal/1180 kJ, 20 g (2 units) carbohydrate, 9 g fibre, 20 g protein, 9 g fat

1 tbsp polyunsaturated oil
200 g/7 oz lean pork, diced
1 medium-sized onion, sliced
1 tbsp wholemeal flour
150 ml/¼ pt chicken or meat stock
150 ml/¼ pt dry red wine
seasoning
½ tsp dried mixed herbs
2 small leeks, sliced
400 g/14 oz courgettes or small marrows, sliced, with skin
1 medium-sized red pepper, sliced into strips
100 g/3½ oz dried peas, soaked (see page 12)
1 hard-boiled egg, chopped
1 tbsp chopped red pepper
2 tbsp chopped parsley

➧

Mont Blanc (top, see p. 60), Celebration Melon (bottom, see p. 60).

Heat the oil in a flameproof casserole. Add the pork and fry gently until it starts to brown. Add the onion and cook until pale golden brown, then sprinkle over the flour and cook for a few minutes, stirring. Remove from the heat and add the stock, stirring. Bring back to the boil and stir in the wine. Add the seasoning and herbs, then the remaining vegetables. Cover and cook slowly for about 1 hour or until all the vegetables are cooked. Garnish with chopped egg, red pepper and parsley and serve straight from the casserole.

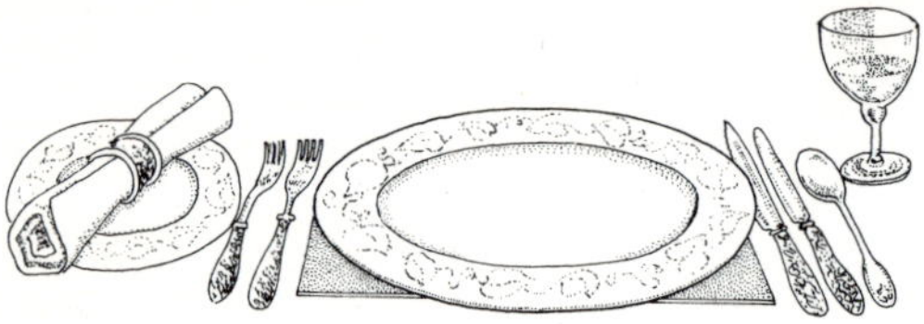

ENTERTAINING

DINNER PARTY DISHES

Bortsch

Serves 4, twice

Each serving: 60 kcal/250 kJ, 10 g (1 unit) carbohydrate, 5 g fibre, 4 g protein, negligible fat

300 g/10½ oz onions, finely chopped
400 g/14 oz raw beetroot, peeled and grated
100 g/3½ oz carrots, diced
100 g/3½ oz celery stalks, chopped
2 litres/3½ pt beef stock
bouquet garni (parsley, bay leaf and thyme)
300 g/10½ oz cabbage, finely shredded
3 tbsp tomato purée
seasoning
2 tbsp vinegar
4 tbsp natural bran flakes
150 ml/¼ pt low-fat plain yoghurt

Put the onions, beetroot, carrots, celery, stock and bouquet garni into a saucepan. Bring to the boil, cover with a tight-fitting lid and simmer gently for 20 minutes. Add the cabbage and continue cooking for a further 20 minutes. Mix in the tomato purée and seasoning and, if necessary, continue cooking until the cabbage is tender. Remove the bouquet garni and stir in the vinegar and bran.

Before serving, put a good spoonful of yoghurt into each plate and add the soup.

Mediterranean fish soup

Serves 8

Each serving: 180 kcal/750 kJ, 30 g (3 units) carbohydrate, 5 g fibre, 13 g protein, 3 g fat

1 tbsp polyunsaturated margarine
2 medium-sized onions, sliced
1 clove garlic, crushed
3 small leeks, cut into rings
1 tbsp tomato purée
2 medium-sized potatoes, halved and sliced
400 g/14 oz canned tomatoes, chopped with juice
finely grated rind of ½ lemon
2 litres/3½ pt chicken stock
bouquet garni (parsley, bay leaf and thyme)
seasoning
150 g/5 oz fresh or frozen sweetcorn kernels
150 g/5 oz wholemeal spaghetti, broken into short lengths
100 g/3½ oz haddock fillet, without bone
100 g/3½ oz cod fillet, without bone
6 tbsp dry white wine
100 g/3½ oz peeled shrimps

Melt the margarine in a large saucepan. Add the onions, garlic and leeks, cover and simmer gently for 5 minutes. Add the tomato purée, potatoes, tomatoes, lemon rind, stock, bouquet garni and seasoning and bring to the boil, stirring occasionally. Add the corn and spaghetti, cover and simmer for 15 minutes.

Cut the haddock and cod into bite-sized pieces, then add to the saucepan with the wine. After 5 minutes, add the shrimps, cover and simmer for a further 5 minutes or until all the fish is cooked. Remove the bouquet garni.

Serve with hot wholemeal garlic bread (made by slicing bread with a knife which has had a clove of garlic rubbed over the surface).

Leeks in red wine

Serves 4

Each serving: 120 kcal/500 kJ, (1 unit) carbohydrate, 8 g fibre, 5 g protein, 4 g fat

1 kg/2¼ lb leeks, sliced into 12 mm/½ in rounds
5 tbsp dry red wine
2 tbsp polyunsaturated oil
¼ tsp salt

Heat the oven to 170°C/325°F/gas 3.

Place the well-rinsed leeks in an ovenproof casserole and add all the ingredients. Cover with greaseproof paper and a tight-fitting lid and cook in the oven for 1–1½ hours, or until the leeks are tender.

If the oven is not required for the main course or other purposes, cook the leeks slowly in a flameproof casserole on top of the stove.

Okra and tomatoes in white wine

Serves 4, twice

Each serving, 60 kcal/250 kJ, negligible (0 units) carbohydrate, 4 g fibre, 2 g protein, 2 g fat

1 tbsp sunflower or other polyunsaturated oil
4 tbsp stock
1 large onion, thinly sliced
1 clove garlic, crushed
450 g/1 lb okra, with stems cut off and blanched
2 medium-sized green peppers, cut into short strips
1–2 tsp paprika
450 g/1 lb tomatoes, chopped
150 ml/¼ pt dry white wine or cider
4 tbsp chopped parsley
salt

Heat the oil with the stock over low heat and fry the onion and garlic gently for 5 minutes until transparent. Add the okra and green pepper strips and sprinkle in the paprika. Cover and cook over low heat for 10 minutes, then stir in the tomatoes, wine, parsley and a little salt. Re-cover and cook over medium heat for a further 10 minutes, or until the vegetables are tender. Serve hot or chilled.

Stuffed rainbow trout

Serves 6

Each serving: 150 kcal/630 kJ, negligible (0 units) carbohydrate, 2 g fibre, 25 g protein, 5 g fat

6 rainbow trout, 200–250 g/7–9 oz each
1 medium-sized red pepper, chopped
1 medium-sized green pepper, chopped
200 g/7 oz button mushrooms, sliced
1 tbsp lemon juice
2 tbsp fresh mixed herbs (parsley, thyme, fennel, chives)
seasoning
lettuce leaves, whole or shredded
mustard and cress
lemon twists

Heat the oven to 180°C/350°F/gas 4.

Clean the fish thoroughly. Put the peppers, mushrooms, lemon juice, herbs and seasoning into a bowl and mix thoroughly. Stuff each trout with the mixture. Place in one layer on a foil-lined ovenproof dish and place any extra stuffing around the fish. Fold the foil over the trout and make an overlap to seal. Bake for about 30 minutes. To serve, arrange the fish on a bed of lettuce and cress and garnish with lemon twists. Accompany with Potato, or other, Salad (see pages 29–30).

Sole Toledo

Serves 4

Each serving: 170 kcal/710 kJ, 10 g (1 unit) carbohydrate, 5 g fibre, 24 g protein, 5 g fat

340 g/12 oz tomatoes, chopped
225 g/8oz button mushrooms, sliced
200 g/7 oz onions, finely chopped
100 g/3½ oz spring onions, chopped
4 tbsp chopped parsley
1 tsp garlic salt
pepper
4 medium-sized sole fillets, skinned
30 g/1 oz low-fat margarine (spread)

Heat the oven to 200°C/400°F/gas 6.

Mix the tomatoes, mushrooms, onions, spring onions, half the parsley and seasoning together. Place the fish in a large, flat, non-stick baking dish and pile the vegetable mixture on top. Dot with the low-fat margarine, cover and bake for 40–45 minutes or until the fish is cooked. Sprinkle with the remaining parsley and serve.

Other white fish fillets may be used instead of sole.

Marengo-style chicken

Serves 4

Each serving: 300 kcal/1260 kJ, 20 g (2 units) carbohydrate, 10 g fibre, 31 g protein, 9 g fat

1 tbsp low-fat margarine (spread)
200 ml/⅓ pt chicken stock
300 g/10½ oz chicken meat, cubed
60 g/2 oz lean bacon, chopped
2 small onions, sliced
1 clove garlic, crushed
2 tbsp wholemeal flour
2 tbsp tomato purée
150 ml/¼ pt dry white wine or cider
bouquet garni (parsley, bay leaf and thyme)
seasoning
4 small tomatoes
200 g/7 oz frozen peas
200 g/7 oz button mushrooms, halved
2 tbsp chopped parsley
1 hard-boiled egg, chopped
12 stoned black olives, halved lengthways
100 g/3½ oz crusty wholemeal bread (4 pieces)

Melt margarine with a few spoonfuls of stock in a flameproof casserole and cook the chicken and bacon until the chicken is lightly browned. Stir in the onions and garlic, cover and simmer gently for about 10 minutes, stirring occasionally. Sprinkle the flour over the ingredients, then stir for a few minutes. Add the remaining stock, stirring slowly. Blend the tomato purée with the wine and add with the bouquet garni and seasoning to the pan. Cover and simmer for about 30 minutes.

Add the tomatoes, peas and mushrooms, return to the simmer and cook for a further 10–15 minutes. Remove the bouquet garni, adjust the seasoning and stir in the parsley. Sprinkle the chopped egg and olives on top and serve straight from the casserole, accompanied by the crusty wholemeal bread.

Pork kebabs

Serves 4
Each serving: 300 kcal/1260 kJ, 40 g (4 units) carbohydrate, 5 g fibre, 16 g protein, 8 g fat

225 g/8 oz lean pork fillet
150 g/5 oz pineapple cubes, canned in natural juice without sugar
12 button onions, parboiled
8 small, firm tomatoes
100 g/3½ oz button mushrooms
400 g/14 oz cooked long-grain brown rice (see page 14)

Sauce for basting
1 tbsp polyunsaturated oil
6 tbsp pineapple juice from can
1 tsp chopped marjoram
1 tbsp chopped parsley
2 tsp Worcester sauce
1 clove garlic, crushed

First, prepare the basting sauce about 2 hours in advance of cooking to allow flavours to blend. Keep in the refrigerator and strain before using. Cut the pork into 20 mm/¾ in cubes and cut each cube in half. Arrange the pork, pineapple cubes, onions, tomatoes and mushrooms on 4 long kebab skewers. Brush the kebabs with the sauce and grill under a medium heat, turning and basting regularly, for 20–25 minutes. Serve on a bed of brown rice, spooning any remaining marinade over the kebabs.

Alternatively, for barbecues omit the brown rice and use pitta bread (wholemeal if possible) to pocket the kebabs.

Chop suey

See page 51

Serves 6 (with Chinese-style Rice, see opposite)
Each serving of Chop Suey: 140 kcal/590 kJ, 10 g (1 unit) carbohydrate, 7 g fibre, 16 g protein, 5 g fat

2 tsp sunflower or other polyunsaturated oil
1 medium-sized onion, chopped
1 clove garlic, crushed
2 medium-sized green peppers, chopped
150 ml/¼pt chicken stock
2 tsp soya sauce, or to taste
400 g/14 oz fresh or canned bean sprouts
200 g/7 oz cooked mung beans (see pages 12–13)
200 g/7 oz cooked chicken, diced
seasoning
1 tbsp wholemeal flour
200 g/7 oz button mushrooms, grilled and sliced

Heat the oil in a non-stick frying pan. Add the onion, garlic and peppers and fry gently for about 5 minutes, stirring occasionally. Add the stock, soya sauce, bean sprouts, mung beans, chicken and seasoning and bring to the boil.

Blend the flour with a little cold water and stir into the mixture. Return to simmering point, stirring constantly, and simmer for 5 minutes or until thickened. Adjust the seasoning if necessary, add the mushrooms and serve with Chinese-style Rice and ½ quantity of Sweet and Sour Sauce (see page 100).

Note
The vegetables, rice and Sweet and Sour Sauce can be prepared beforehand, covered and kept in the refrigerator until required. The dishes themselves could be cooked in advance and left in the pans for quick reheating when guests arrive.

If more than 6 people are to have this meal, double the amount of Chop Suey and/or Chinese Rice stated in the recipe or serve an extra bowl of cooked brown rice or noodles (see pages 14 and 15) or cook some Chinese Bean Sprouts and Radishes, or Crisp Vegetable Fry (see page 33).

Chinese-style rice

See page 51

Serves 6 (with Chop Suey, above)
Each serving of Chinese-style Rice: 160 kcal/670 kJ, 20 g (2 units) carbohydrate, 3 g fibre, 8 g protein, 4 g fat

1 egg, beaten
2 tsp sunflower or other polyunsaturated oil
1 medium-sized onion, chopped
400 g/14 oz long-grain brown rice, cooked in chicken stock (see page 14)
100 g/3½ oz lean ham, cut into strips
6 spring onions, green and white, finely chopped
2 tsp Worcester sauce or soya sauce, or to taste
seasoning
100 g/3½ oz pineapple canned without sugar, chopped
3 tbsp Soy Nuts (see page 67), lightly crushed

Use a non-stick frying pan to make a thin omelette with the egg, shred into strips and reserve.

Heat the oil in a large non-stick frying pan. Add the onion and fry gently until golden brown. Add the rice, ham and spring onions and cook quickly for a further 5 minutes, stirring. Add the Worcester sauce and seasoning then the pineapple, Soy Nuts and egg. Heat through and serve as an accompaniment to Chop Suey, above.

Garnish
You can make decorative garnishes from most vegetables. The photograph on page 51 shows carrot feathers, a cucumber fan and tomato concertinas.

Celebration melon

See page 52

Serves 6

Each serving: 40 kcal/170 kJ, 10 g (1 unit) carbohydrate, 5 g fibre, 1 g protein, 0 g fat

1 large honeydew melon
100 g/3½ oz fresh or frozen strawberries
100 g/3½ oz fresh or frozen raspberries
100 g/3½ oz pineapple, canned without sugar
100 g/3½ oz fresh or frozen loganberries
100 g/3½ oz fresh or frozen red currants
100 g/3½ oz black or green grapes
3 tbsp brandy or pure kirsch (optional)
sugar-free sweetener to taste

Cut the melon in half lengthways and remove the seeds. Scoop out the flesh with a melon baller or cut into small pieces. Prepare the fruit and mix with the melon balls, juice from the canned pineapple, brandy/kirsch, if using, and sweetener. Chill until required.

To serve: if necessary, cut a little skin from the undersides of the melon to make the halves sit properly on a large serving dish. Pile the fruit mixture into the shells, garnishing with a few reserved pieces of fruit, if liked. Serve with home-made Orange Sorbet (see page 88).

Mont Blanc

See page 52

Serves 6

Each serving: 190 kcal/800 kJ, 50 g (5 units) carbohydrate, 5 g fibre, 6 g protein, 5 g fat

450 g/1 lb skinned chestnuts
450 ml/¾ pt skimmed milk
2 tbsp brandy
sugar-free sweetener to taste
300 ml/½ pt Cream Substitute I (see page 89)

Cook the chestnuts gently in the milk for about 45 minutes, or until they are tender and all the milk has been absorbed. Pipe, or rub through a coarse sieve or baby Mouli *directly* on to a flat serving dish. Try to avoid breaking up the vermicelli-like sieved shreds of chestnut – it should be light and fluffy. Alternatively, purée in a blender, although the classic vermicelli-like shreds will not be achieved. Allow to cool slightly, then pile up gently, into a pyramid shape using a wet knife. Add the brandy and sweetener to the Cream Substitute and place on top of the peak using a knife to make it look like snowdrifts. Serve, if possible, within the hour.

Caribbean rumba

Serves 8
Each serving: 90 kcal/380 kJ, 10 g (1 unit) carbohydrate, 2 g fibre, 4 g protein, 2 g fat

300 g/10½ oz ripe peeled bananas
100 g/3½ oz fresh pineapple or canned without sugar
2 tbsp lemon juice
2 tbsp rum
150 ml/¼ pt well-chilled evaporated milk
3 tsp gelatine dissolved in 4 tbsp hot water
2 tbsp flaked almonds, toasted and finely chopped
sugar-free sweetener equivalent to 60 g/4 tbsp sugar

Purée the banana and pineapple together in a blender and stir in the lemon juice and rum. Whisk the milk and the dissolved gelatine together and fold into the fruit purée, with the chopped almonds and sweetener. Pour into freezer trays and freeze without stirring.

Alternatively, the ice cream can be frozen in a mould and, when turned out, decorated with fruit such as red currants, dessert cherries on the stalk or strawberries.

FESTIVE FARE

Birthday cheesecake

Serves 12
Each serving: 100 kcal/420 kJ, 10 g (1 unit) carbohydrate, 5 g fibre, 6 g protein, 3 g fat

125 g/4½ oz wholemeal breadcrumbs
2 tbsp natural bran flakes
1 tsp ground cinnamon
60 g/2 oz low-fat margarine (spread)
200 g/7 oz skimmed milk curd cheese
300 ml/½ pt low-fat plain yoghurt
100 ml/3½ fl oz fresh orange juice
sugar-free sweetener to taste
3 tsp gelatine dissolved in 4 tbsp hot water
450 g /1 lb fresh or frozen raspberries
1 egg white, whisked
225 g/8 oz large strawberries, halved
1 tbsp brandy or pure kirsch (optional, omit for children)

Toast the breadcrumbs and mix with the bran, cinnamon and low-fat spread. Press into the base of a 23–25 cm/9–10 in flan tin and leave to cool. Mix the cheese, yoghurt, orange juice and sweetener together. Blend the dissolved gelatine into the cheese mixture. Add the raspberries, fold in the egg white and pour the mixture on to the base. Leave in the refrigerator until set.

Meanwhile, sprinkle the strawberries with the brandy and set aside, turning occasionally, while the cheesecake is setting. Decorate the top of the cake with these strawberries before serving.

Birthday or Christmas fruit cake

Makes 12 slices See page 70

Each slice: 180 kcal/760 kJ, 20 g (2 units) carbohydrate, 4 g fibre, 5 g protein, 9 g fat

200 g/7 oz wholemeal self-raising flour, sifted
¼ tsp salt
100 g/3½ oz low-fat margarine (spread)
150 g/5 oz mixed seedless raisins and sultanas, chopped
60 g/2 oz ground almonds
60 g/2 oz ground hazelnuts or hazelnuts, finely chopped
finely grated rind of 1 orange
200 g/7 oz carrots, finely grated
½ tsp mixed spice
¼ tsp ground cinnamon
sugar-free sweetener equivalent to 120 g/4 oz sugar
2 eggs, beaten
3 tbsp orange juice
2 tbsp brandy or rum (optional)

Heat the oven to 180°C/350°F/gas 4.

Mix the flour and salt together and rub in the margarine until the mixture resembles fine breadcrumbs. Add the fruit, nuts, orange rind, carrots and spices, and mix well. Mix the sweetener into the eggs and beat into the dry ingredients. Add enough orange juice to make a soft dough. Put the mixture into a 20 cm/8 in round or 18 cm/7 in square non-stick baking tin and bake for 45–60 minutes. When ready, the cake should be firm to the touch and a warm skewer inserted into the centre should come out clean. If lightly browned, but insufficiently cooked, cover the top with a piece of foil or greaseproof paper and continue cooking until the skewer comes out clean. Cool in the tin. Turn out upside down, make a few skewer holes in the bottom and spoon in any left-over orange juice and spirits if using. Store in an airtight container.

A wider, thinner cake can be made by using a larger shallower tin and reducing the cooking time. A large square tin could be used to make a slab cake, suitable for cutting into squares when cold.

If you want to ice the cake, follow the recipe opposite.

Icing

See page 70

Total recipe: 160 kcal/670 kJ, 25 g (2½ units) carbohydrate, 4 g fibre, 13 g protein, 2 g fat

*200 g/7 oz peeled, cored and sliced, sweet eating apples**
1 tsp powdered gelatine dissolved in 4 tbsp hot water
60 g/2 oz quark or other skimmed milk curd cheese
colouring (optional)

Cook the apples to a soft pulp in a little water and allow to cool. Place in a blender with the dissolved gelatine, cheese and colouring, if used, and blend to a smooth purée. Leave to set, then spread on the cake, and pipe if desired.

This spread, covered, keeps well in the refrigerator and may be deep-frozen.

Suggested uses

Child's birthday cake Spread Birthday Fruit Cake (opposite) with icing when cold. Non-edible candle-holders and other decorations could also be used.

Children's party slab cake Use the same recipe as opposite, but bake in a larger square or oblong tin to give a thinner cake. When cold, cut into squares and decorate each square with a blob of icing topped with a piece of fruit such as a section of mandarin or brightly coloured summer fruit.

Christmas or other celebration cake Use the same recipe as opposite and decorate with seasonal or appropriate non-edible decorations

Low-calorie spread Use on plain biscuits, scones, popovers and so on (5 kcal/20 kJ in 2 tsp).

Plum pudding

See page 70

Serves 8
Each serving: 220 kcal/920 kJ, 30 g (3 units) carbohydrate, 5 g fibre, 5 g protein, 8 g fat

115 g/4 oz wholemeal breadcrumbs
100 g/3½ oz wholemeal flour
1 tsp baking powder
150 g/5 oz dried mixed fruit
grated rind and juice of 1 small orange
grated rind and juice of 1 lemon
2 tsp mixed spice
½ tsp grated nutmeg
½ tsp ground cinnamon
½ tsp salt
200 g/7 oz carrots, grated

*Choose a variety such as Golden Delicious, which stays white when cooked.

100 g/3½ oz cooking apples, grated
150 ml/¼ pt skimmed milk
sugar-free sweetener equivalent to 75 g/5 tbsp sugar
4 tbsp polyunsaturated margarine
1 tsp liquid gravy browning
1 egg, beaten
2 + 2 tbsp brandy or other spirits
1 tsp polyunsaturated margarine (to grease)

Mix all the dry ingredients together and add the carrots, and apples. Put the milk, sweetener, margarine and gravy browning into a small saucepan and warm gently until the margarine has melted. Cool and add to the dry ingredients along with the fruit juice, egg and 2 tbsp brandy. Mix well together. Pour into a greased basin, cover with a lid or foil and steam for 5 hours. Allow to cool, cover with foil and store in a cool dry place. Use within 7–10 days. Steam for 2 hours on the day the pudding is required. To serve, warm 2 tbsp reserved brandy in a large serving spoon or ladle, ignite and pour over pudding. The flamed pudding may be served with Clear Brandy Sauce (see below) or a sugar-free egg custard sauce, flavoured with brandy.

Clear brandy sauce

Serves 8
Each serving: 50 kcal/210 kJ, negligible (0 units) carbohydrate, fibre, protein and fat

2 tbsp cornflour
450 ml/¾ pt boiling water
150 ml/¼ pt brandy
sugar-free sweetener equivalent to 15 g/1 tbsp sugar

Blend the cornflour with a little cold water and stir into the boiling water. Boil for 2–3 minutes, stirring. Remove from the heat and add brandy and sweetener. Serve with Plum Pudding (above).

Hot cross buns

Makes 7
Each bun: 140 kcal/590 kJ, 20 g (2 units) carbohydrate, 3 g fibre, 5 g protein 4 g fat

1 tsp sugar
6 tbsp lukewarm skimmed milk
1½ tsp dried yeast or 15 g/½ oz fresh yeast
170 g/6 oz wholemeal flour
1 tsp salt
1 tsp mixed spice
30 g/1 oz sultanas
1 tsp grated orange rind (optional)
1 tbsp polyunsaturated margarine
1 egg, beaten
1tbsp skimmed milk
30 g/1 oz wholemeal flour as pastry (see page 90)

Heat the oven to 220°C/425°F/gas 7.

Dissolve the sugar in the lukewarm milk, stir into the yeast and leave in a warm place for 10–15 minutes until frothy. Mix the flour with the salt, spice, sultanas and orange rind, if using, in a large bowl and rub in the margarine. Add the yeast liquid to the beaten egg and beat into the flour to form a light, soft dough (a little liquid should remain). Turn on to a lightly floured surface and knead until firm and elastic. Place the dough in a bowl, cover with lightly oiled polythene and leave to rise in a warm place until doubled in size (1–1½ hours). Turn the dough on to a lightly floured surface and knead for about 2 minutes until firm. Form into balls, place on a warmed non-stick baking tin and cover. Allow to rise for 20–30 minutes, until twice their original size. Brush with the remaining egg and milk and place a cross of uncooked pastry on top. Bake for about 20 minutes or until the buns have risen and are brown. Serve warm.

PARTY SNACKS

Diabetics who are used to estimating the permitted quantities of controlled foods by sight will be able to help themselves to suitable amounts. If you are not able to do this, ask your dietician or doctor for advice.

Dips

See page 69

Dips should be the consistency of really thick cream, and should be well seasoned. A blender is useful for preparing basic dips, but it is better to add flavourings, finely chopped after. Retain 1–2 tsp of the distinctive ingredients to garnish. Prepare in advance and serve in bowls at room temperature.

Suitable foods for dipping
Piles of different coloured fresh vegetables cut into sticks – for example, small carrots, celery, cucumber, swede, large red and green peppers. Wholemeal bread sticks (halved). For a large party, try a Catherine wheel of wholemeal bread to break off strips.

On cocktail sticks
Black, green and stuffed olives, gherkins, cocktail onions, cubes of tomato, melon, pineapple, grilled mushroom. Savoury cottage cheese balls, small strips of curled lean ham, rolled anchovy fillets and bite-sized pieces of curried chicken. Mixed combinations of the above may also be used.

Basic soft cheese dip

Total 300 ml/½ pt: 240 kcal/1010 kJ, 10 g (1 unit) carbohydrate, 0 g fibre, 30 g protein, 9 g fat

200 g/7 oz skimmed milk curd cheese or sieved cottage cheese
100 ml/3½ fl oz low-fat plain yoghurt
seasoning

Blend or mash the cheese and yoghurt together, season well then add finely chopped ingredients, which add fibre, to give one of the following variations:

Variations

Salad dip 3 spring onions; 1 small green pepper; 5 cm/2 in cucumber, with skin; 1 clove garlic, crushed; 2 tbsp chopped fresh parsley and thyme.

Tomato dip 2 tbsp tomato purée; 2 tbsp low-calorie tomato ketchup; 1 small red pepper; 1 small onion; ½ tsp curry powder.

Devil's dip 1 small onion; 2 tbsp mustard pickle; 2 tbsp vinegar; 1 tsp curry powder; 1 hard-boiled egg (to garnish); paprika (to garnish).

Pickle dip 1 tbsp unsweetened pickle; 2–3 gherkins; 1 tbsp capers; 6 cocktail onions; 1 small green pepper (to garnish).

Mustard dip 1 tbsp French mustard or to taste; 2 tbsp low-calorie salad cream; Worcester sauce to taste; pinch fresh or dried mixed herbs; 1 punnet mustard and cress (to garnish).

Bean and bacon dip

See page 69

Total: 670 kcal/2810 kJ, 90 g (9 units) carbohydrate, 25 g fibre, 60 g protein, 12 g fat

425 g/15 oz butter beans canned without sugar, or cooked beans (see pages 12–13)
60 g/2 oz skimmed milk curd cheese
4 tbsp low-fat plain yoghurt
100 g/3½ oz spring onions, finely chopped
¼ tsp tabasco sauce or to taste
seasoning
100 g/3½ oz lean bacon, grilled and chopped

Mash or blend together the beans, cheese and yoghurt. Stir in the spring onions, tabasco sauce and seasoning and pour into a serving bowl. Serve at room temperature with the finely chopped bacon sprinkled over the top.

Barbecue dip

Use the Barbecue Sauce recipe on page 98, making sure it is well simmered down to a thick creamy consistency. Serve hot or cold.

Cocktail canapés

See page 69

These should be bite sized, well flavoured and attractive to look at. They should be easy to pick up in the fingers. Diabetics who are used to estimating the permitted quantities of controlled foods by sight will be able to help themselves to suitable amounts.

Suitable bases

Try small squares or circles of wholemeal toast or rye bread, bought wholemeal biscuits or pieces of crispbread, or bite-sized wholemeal Pancakes (see page 75).

For spreading on the bases try thinly spread skimmed milk curd cheese, salad dressing (see pages 101–2), pâtés (see pages 20–1) or low-fat margarine (spread) mixed with other flavourings such as anchovy essence or a speck of French mustard.

Toppings

Small leftover scraps from the refrigerator can go a surprisingly long way – for example, small pieces of chicken, canned fish or lean ham. Most delicatessens stock a whole range of suitable toppings and will sell thin slivers of smoked fish by the ounce or small pots of mock caviare. Vegetables can be used on their own – for example, mushrooms which have been poached in a little wine, or neat slices of tomato.

Decoration

Use small pieces of coloured salad vegetables, sliced olives, cocktail onions or sliced gherkins to add colour.

Soy nuts

See page 69

Each 30 g/3 tbsp: 120 kcal/500 kJ, 10 g (1 unit) carbohydrate, 4 g fibre, 11 g protein, 5 g fat

Soak about 225–450 g/½–1 lb of soya beans overnight. Drain and towel dry. Place on a baking sheet and cook in a moderate oven (170°C/325°F/gas3) until the beans are crispy all the way through – they will shrink back to their original size. Cool and store in an airtight container.

As well as being eaten as nibbles to accompany drinks, they can be added whole, ground or crushed to breakfast cereals, bread dough and other baking mixtures, or sprinkled over salads and snacks.

Chick nuts*

Each 30 g/3 tbsp: 110 kcal/460 kJ, 20 g (2 units) carbohydrate, 8 g fibre, 6 g protein, 2 g fat

Chick nuts as nibbles

Make as Soy Nuts above using soaked chick peas.

Chick devils

Sprinkle lightly, then toss the baked nuts in a mixture of cayenne pepper and salt while still hot. A few drops of lemon juice may be added.

Red chicks

Sprinkle lightly and then toss the baked 'nuts' with paprika and garlic salt.

PARTY DRINKS

White wine cup

Serves 6

Total recipe: 760 kcal/3190 kJ, negligible (0 units) carbohydrate, fibre, protein and fat

300 ml/½ pt boiling water
pared rind of 1 orange
1 small cinnamon stick
small sprig of borage (optional)
3 cloves
1 miniature bottle brandy
1 litre/1¾ pt dry white wine
sugar-free sweetener to taste
ice cubes

Decoration
Fruits in season such as sliced peach, apple, strawberries, raspberries, and so on.

Pour the boiling water over the orange rind, cinnamon, borage (if used) and cloves and allow to infuse for about 30 minutes. Strain, and add the brandy when really cold. Stir into the wine in a large jug or bowl and sweeten slightly. Add a few ice cubes and the fruit just before serving.

---

*The large white variety are most suitable.

Bean and Bacon Dip (top left, see p. 66), Soy Nuts (see p. 67) and Chick Nuts (top right), White Wine Cup, Cocktail Canapes (bottom, see p. 67).

Mulled wine

Serves 6

Total: 600 kcal/2500 kJ, negligible (0 units) carbohydrate, fibre, protein and fat

pared rind of 1 lemon
pared rind of 1 orange
6 cloves
1 cinnamon stick
300 ml/½ pt boiling water
1 litre/1¾ pt dry red wine
sugar-free sweetener to taste
grated nutmeg

Place the rinds, cloves, cinnamon and water in a saucepan. Bring to the boil, cover and allow to infuse away from the heat for about 30 minutes. Strain into a large saucepan and add the wine. Heat until hot but not boiling. Add the sweetener and transfer to a heated serving bowl. Just before serving, grate a little nutmeg over the surface. Serve in warmed glasses.

Summer fruit punch

Serves 6

Each serving: 60 kcal/250 kJ, 10 g (1 unit) carbohydrate, negligible fibre, protein and fat

450 ml/¾ pt unsweetened orange juice
300 ml/½ pt unsweetened grapefruit juice
juice of 2 lemons
sugar-free sweetener to taste
pared rind of 1 lemon
850 ml/1½ pt chilled soda water

Decoration
slices of orange, lemon and colourful summer fruits

Place the fruit juices, sweetener and the lemon rind in a large basin, add the fruits used for decoration and chill.

To serve, remove the lemon rind and transfer the fruit and juices to a punch bowl. Add the soda water at the last minute before serving.

Pineapple cooler

Serves 6

Each serving: 110 kcal/460 kJ, 20 g (2 units) carbohydrate, negligible fibre, 4 g protein, 1 g fat

450 ml/¾ pt low-fat plain yoghurt
600 ml/1 pt unsweetened pineapple juice
sugar-free sweetener to taste

➧

Plum Pudding (top, see p. 63), Christmas Fruit Cake with Icing (bottom, see pp. 62–3).

Mix all the ingredients together and chill well. Serve in tall glasses, decorated with a few pieces of fresh fruit such as sliced strawberries or sprigs of cherries on the tumbler rim.

Sparkling cider cup

Serves 8
Each serving: 70 kcal/290 kJ, 10 g (1 unit) carbohydrate, negligible fibre, protein and fat

300 ml/½ pt unsweetened canned orange juice, chilled
200 ml/⅓ pt unsweetened pineapple juice, chilled
1 litre/1¾ pt dry cider, chilled
600 ml/1 pt low-calorie sparkling lemon drink, chilled

Decoration
ice cubes, with a fresh cherry or other red fruit frozen in cube

Mix the fruit juices together in a large serving bowl and stir in the cider. Put ice cubes in each tumbler. Add the sparkling lemon to the cider mix, pour over the ice cubes and serve.

COOKING FOR CHILDREN

Most of the analyses in this section are given for the total recipe, rather than for each serving. This has been done because children of different ages eat varying-sized portions. If you are in doubt about how to use these analyses, consult your dietician or doctor.

Spaghetti with meat balls and tomato sauce

Makes 20 small meat balls
Total recipe: 1360 kcal/5710 kJ, 170 g (17 units) carbohydrate, 44 g fibre, 93 g protein, 37 g fat

20 meat balls alone: 590 kcal/2480 kJ, 50 g (5 units) carbohydrate, 24 g fibre, 66 g protein, 17 g fat

200 g/7 oz cooked butter beans (see pages 12–13)
200 g/7 oz lean beef, finely minced
3 tbsp wholemeal breadcrumbs
4 tbsp natural bran flakes
onion salt
pepper
good pinch ground mace (optional)
1 egg, beaten
450 ml/¾ pt Tomato Sauce (see page 100)
510 g/18 oz cooked wholemeal spaghetti (see page 15)

Mash the beans with a fork and mix in the meat, breadcrumbs, bran, seasoning, mace, if using, and the egg. Shape into 20 very small meat balls. Arrange in the grill pan and cook under a medium-hot grill, turning until well browned all over. When cooked, serve in the Tomato Sauce with the spaghetti (see page 15).

Variations
The meat balls can be served hot or cold, with or without the sauce and with or without the spaghetti.

Flavourings such as chopped vegetables, herbs and spices can be added to the meat according to taste.

Other types of lean meats (e.g. liver) can be incorporated.

Chopped tomatoes, red peppers or other acceptable vegetables can be added to the sauce. Different varieties of wholemeal pasta can be substituted for the spaghetti.

Chicken and summer vegetables

Total recipe: 1000 kcal/4200 kJ, 60 g (6 units) carbohydrate, 36 g fibre, 115 g protein, 36 g fat

1 tbsp polyunsaturated oil
1 shallot or small onion, chopped
450 g/1 lb chicken meat (4 portions)
200 ml/⅓ pt chicken stock
seasoning
100 g/3½ oz carrots, diced
100 g/3½ oz fresh or frozen peas
100 g/3½ oz sweetcorn kernels
200 g/7 oz cooked beans (see pages 12–13)
gravy browning (optional)

Heat the oil in a flameproof casserole. Add the shallot and fry gently until golden brown. Add the chicken and brown on both sides. Add the chicken stock, seasoning and carrots, cover and cook for 1 hour. Add the peas and corn and simmer for a further 10 minutes or until the chicken and vegetables are tender. Remove from the heat and strain off the liquid from the casserole. Add to the beans and purée in a blender. Add the bean mixture with gravy browning, if using, to the casserole, return to the simmer, uncovered, and simmer until heated through. Serve with potatoes in their skin, brown rice or wholemeal pasta.

Chilli con carne with baked beans

Total recipe: 720 kcal/3020 kJ, 60 g (6 units) carbohydrate, 34 g fibre, 65 g protein, 27 g fat

1 tbsp polyunsaturated oil
1 large onion, chopped
2 medium-sized red peppers, diced
200 g/7 oz lean meat, minced
4–6 tbsp stock
400 g/14 oz baked beans
½–2 tsp chilli powder
seasoning

Heat the oil in a saucepan. Add the onion, peppers and meat and fry gently for 5 minutes, stirring occasionally. Mix in the stock and simmer for a further 10 minutes. Add the beans and chilli powder, stirring well. Cook for a further 10 minutes, adjust the seasoning and serve.

Instead of using one kind of meat, a mixture including, for example, minced liver, kidney or lean ham, may be used.

Cottage pie

Total recipe: 910 kcal/3820 kJ, 130 g (13 units) carbohydrate, 26 g fibre, 84 g protein, 10 g fat

200 g/7 oz lean cooked meat
250 g/9 oz cooked haricot or other beans (see pages 12–13)
1 medium-sized boiled onion
100 ml/3½ fl oz stock or gravy
2–3 tbsp low-calorie ketchup
seasoning
4 tbsp skimmed milk
400 g/14 oz mashed potatoes

Heat the oven to 200°C/400°F/gas 6.

Mince the meat, beans and onion together. Mix thoroughly with the stock, ketchup and seasoning and place in a pie dish. Add the milk to the potatoes, season well and cover the pie. Bake in the oven for about 30 minutes or until well browned.

Fish cakes

Makes 8

Total recipe: 700 kcal/2940 kJ, 80 g (8 units) carbohydrate, 29 g fibre, 69 g protein, 13 g fat

200 g/7 oz poached white fish, flaked
100 g/3½ oz freshly mashed potatoes
200 g/7 oz cooked butter beans (see pages 12–13) mashed
2 tbsp chopped parsley
1 tbsp low-calorie tomato ketchup
2 tsp Worcester sauce
½ tsp onion salt

Coating
45 g/1½ oz wholemeal breadcrumbs
4 tbsp natural bran flakes
1 egg, beaten

Heat the oven to 220°C/425°F/gas 7.

Mix all the non-coating ingredients together and store in the refrigerator until cold (about 30 minutes). Roll into a long cylinder and cut into 8 flat rounds or other shapes. To coat, mix the crumbs and bran together in a polythene bag. One at a time, dip the cakes into the egg then shake gently in the bag, pressing the crumbs firmly into the cakes. Place on a non-stick ovenproof dish and bake in the oven for 15–20 minutes until golden brown. Alternatively, cook on each side under a medium grill.

Tomatoes, sprinkled with a little salt, could be baked at the same time as the fish cakes.

Pancakes

Makes 8

Each pancake: 70 kcal/290 kJ, 10 g (1 unit) carbohydrate, 1 g fibre, 4 g protein, 2 g fat

100 g/3½ oz wholemeal flour
¼ tsp salt
1 egg
1 egg white
300 ml/½ pt skimmed milk
1 tsp polyunsaturated oil

Place the flour and salt in a bowl, make a well in the centre and drop in the egg and egg white. Gradually add ⅓ of the milk, beating until smooth. Stir in the remaining milk and the oil, transfer to a jug, cover and set aside for 30 minutes. Stir before using.

Use a good quality non-stick frying pan measuring 15–17 cm/6–7 in. Make the pancakes in the usual way, using a small ladle to transfer the batter to the pan. Stack flat until ready to serve.

Orange pancakes

See page 79

Makes 8

Each pancake: 80 kcal/340 kJ, 10 g (1 unit) carbohydrate, 2 g fibre, 4 g protein, 2 g fat

basic batter, as in Pancakes above
finely grated rind of 1 large orange
sugar-free sweetener equivalent to 15 g/1 tbsp sugar
1 large orange
8 tsp sugar-free orange marmalade

Add to the basic batter the grated orange rind and the sugar-free sweetener, and make as above.

Spread each pancake with a teaspoonful of sugar-free orange marmalade, and fold over. Slice the orange into thin half-slices and serve on top of the pancakes.

Blackberry pancakes

Makes 8
Each pancake: 90 kcal/380 kJ, 10 g (1 unit) carbohydrate, 3 g fibre, 6 g protein, 2 g fat

basic batter, as in Pancakes above
200 g/7 oz fresh or frozen blackberries, crushed
100 g/3½ oz skimmed milk curd cheese

Make the batter and pancakes as on page 75. Fill with blackberries mixed with skimmed milk curd cheese. Decorate with a few whole reserved blackberries.

Ice creams

- ☐ Turn the refrigerator control to the coldest level
- ☐ Made in advance ice creams will keep their flavour for a month if stored in the deep-freeze.
- ☐ Allow 2–4 hours for the complete freezing process. Several factors cause time variations.
- ☐ Allow ice cream to soften slightly in the main compartment of the refrigerator for 1–1½ hours before serving.
- ☐ Gelatine is added to sugar-free ice creams to give smoothness and to help prevent the formation of ice crystals.
- ☐ 100 g/3½ oz of fruit yields approximately 50 ml/1⅔ fl oz of purée.

Vanilla ice cream

Serves 8
Each serving: 60 kcal/250 kJ, 5 g (½ unit) carbohydrate, 0 g fibre, 4 g protein, 3 g fat

2 tsp gelatine dissolved in 2 tbsp hot water
300 ml/½ pt well-chilled evaporated milk
1 tsp vanilla essence
sugar-free sweetener equivalent to 60 g/4 tbsp sugar

Whisk the milk and almost cold gelatine together and add the flavouring and sweetener. Pour into freezing trays and freeze without stirring. Serve with fruit or fruit purée.

Coffee ice cream

See pages 80–1

Serves 8
Each serving: as Vanilla Ice Cream

Make as for Vanilla Ice Cream, adding 1½–2 tbsp instant coffee dissolved in 3 tbsp of the milk, then whisked into the milk mixture.

4 Toms. chicken

Parsley

P57 Marengo-style Chicken

Cape Bredie P50 LAMB

2 x 400gm Black eye beans.

P49 Steak & kidney hot pot Beef

Celery

200gm red kidney beans

~~stewing steak?~~

P48 2 x 400 gm butter beans

Mexican beef paprika

Celery 3 peppers ?

THE TIMES

Yesterdays Solution — Mild

2	1	6	3	7	9	5	4	8
8	4	3	2	6	5	1	9	7
9	7	5	8	4	1	6	3	2
1	9	7	4	8	6	2	5	3
6	5	2	1	9	3	8	7	4
3	8	4	5	2	7	9	1	6
5	6	8	9	3	4	7	2	1
4	2	1	7	5	8	3	6	9
7	3	9	6	1	2	4	8	5

su doku

NOVEMBER

M	T	W	T	F	S	S
				1	2	3
4	5	6	7	8	9	10
11	12	13	14	15	16	17
18	19	20	21	22	23	24
25	26	27	28	29	30	

Difficult

9	4	7	2	3	6	1	5	8
1	8	2	9	4	5	3	6	7
3	5	6	8	7	1	9	4	2
2	3	9	4	5	7	6	8	1
5	6	1	3	8	2	7	9	4
8	7	4	6	1	9	2	3	5
6	1	8	7	9	4	5	2	3
7	9	3	5	2	8	4	1	6
4	2	5	1	6	3	8	7	9

Strawberry ice cream

See pages 80–1

Serves 8

Each serving: 40 kcal/170 kJ, 5 g (½ unit) carbohydrate, 1 g fibre, 3 g protein, 2 g fat

340 g/12 oz fresh or frozen strawberries
150 ml/¼ pt well-chilled evaporated milk
2 tsp gelatine dissolved in 2 tbsp hot water
sugar-free sweetener equivalent to 60 g/4 tbsp sugar

Reserve a few pieces of fruit for decoration. Purée the remainder in a blender (do not sieve strawberries as this removes the fibre). Whisk the milk and the almost cold gelatine together, add the sweetener and fold in the purée. Pour into freezing trays and freeze without stirring.

Raspberry ice cream

Serves 8

Each serving: 40 kcal/170 kJ, 5 g (½ unit) carbohydrate, 3 g fibre, 3 g protein, 2 g fat

Make as for Strawberry Ice Cream above, using raspberries.

Banana ice cream

Serves 8

Each serving: 60 kcal/250 kJ, 10 g (1 unit) carbohydrate, 1 g fibre, 3 g protein, 2 g fat

300 g/10½ oz very ripe peeled bananas
2 tbsp lemon juice
2 tsp gelatine dissolved in 2 tbsp hot water
150 ml/¼ pt well-chilled evaporated milk
sugar-free sweetener equivalent to 60 g/4 tbsp sugar

Reserve a small banana and 1 tbsp lemon juice. Mash the remainder to a purée and continue as for Strawberry Ice Cream above. Decorate with reserved banana, sliced dipped in lemon juice.

Orange sorbet baskets

See pages 80–1

Follow the recipe for Orange Sorbet on page 88 and spoon the frozen mixture into the shells of 4 orange halves. Make the handles with strips of orange rind.

Raspberry pudding

Serves 4

Each serving: 120 kcal/500 kJ, 20 g (2 units) carbohydrate, 5 g fibre, 9 g protein, negligible fat

600 ml/1 pt skimmed milk
3 tbsp wholemeal semolina
sugar-free sweetener to taste
225 g/8 oz fresh or frozen raspberries
1 tsp polyunsaturated margarine (to grease)

Heat the oven to 200°C/400°F/gas 6.

Heat the milk, sprinkle in the semolina and, stirring all the time, bring slowly to the boil. Continue stirring at simmering point until the grain is soft (about 10 minutes). Remove from the heat and add the sweetener. Divide the raspberries between 4 individual greased baking dishes, then pour over the semolina mixture. Bake in the oven for about 20 minutes until lightly browned. May be made into one pudding.

Gingerbread men

Total recipe: 1690 kcal/7100 kJ, 160 g (16 units) carbohydrate, 63 g fibre, 47 g protein, 100 g fat

200 g/7 oz self-raising wholemeal flour
¼ tsp salt
1 tsp bicarbonate of soda
100 g/3½ oz natural bran flakes
3 tsp ground ginger, or to taste
1 tsp mixed spice
1 tsp ground cinnamon
100 g/3½ oz polyunsaturated margarine
sugar-free sweetener equivalent to 90 g/6 tbsp sugar
1 egg, beaten
3 tbsp orange juice
1 tsp polyunsaturated margarine (to grease)

Heat the oven to 180°C/350°F/gas 4.

Mix the flour, salt, bicarbonate of soda, bran and spices together, then rub in the margarine until the mixture resembles fine breadcrumbs. Stir the sweetener into the egg and orange juice and beat into the flour mixture. Knead well, and roll out thinly on a floured board. Using a cutter, cut into gingerbread men shapes and place on greased baking trays. Bake for 15–20 minutes, or until crisp and lightly browned. Cool on a wire tray and store in an airtight container.

Other shapes can be made – animals, horseshoes and so on.

Gingerbread Men (top), Orange Pancakes (bottom, see p. 75).

Ginger squares

Makes 36

Each square: 50 kcal/210 kJ, 5 g (½ unit) carbohydrate, 2 g fibre, 1 g protein, 3 g fat

Use the mixture for Gingerbread Men above and prepare in the same way, dividing into 36 equal-sized pieces.

Apricot boats

See pages 80–1

Makes 20

Each boat: 90 kcal/370 kJ, 10 g (1 unit) carbohydrate, 2 g fibre, 3 g protein, 3 g fat

200 g/7 oz wholemeal flour
pinch salt
70 g/2½ oz polyunsaturated margarine
100 g/3½ oz cooked mashed potatoes

Filling
200 g/7 oz skimmed milk curd cheese
100 g/3½ oz dried apricots, cooked and puréed
300 ml/½ pt orange jelly

Heat the oven to 200°C/400°F/gas 6.

To make the pastry, mix the flour and salt together and rub in the margarine until the mixture resembles fine breadcrumbs. Knead in the mashed potatoes until a stiff dough is formed. Roll out between sheets of greaseproof paper and cut to fit oval-shaped tartlet tins. Bake blind for 10–15 minutes. Leave to cool. Divide the cheese between the boats and spoon the apricot purée on top. Spoon 1 tbsp jelly, which should be just starting to set, over each tartlet.

To make sailing boats, make mast heads with cocktail sticks spearing triangular paper sails and insert into the filled tartlet cases. On special occasions, serve on a mirror (a lake) with a suitable surrounding.

PREVIOUS SPREAD: Strawberry Ice Cream (top left, see p. 77), Coffee Ice Cream (top centre, see p. 76), Orange Sorbet Baskets (top right and bottom left, see p. 77), Apricot Boats (bottom right, see above). OPPOSITE: Blackcurrant Charlotte (top, see p. 88), Fromage Blanc and Fruit (centre right, see p. 86), Loganberry Cheesecake (bottom, see p. 86).

DESSERTS

Caribbean baked bananas

Serves 4

Each serving: 100 kcal/420 kJ, 20 g (2 units) carbohydrate, 3 g fibre, 1 g protein, negligible fat

4 medium-sized peeled bananas
2 tbsp lemon juice or low-calorie lime squash
juice of 2 oranges
2 tbsp rum, or rum flavouring to taste
pinch ground cinnamon
finely grated rind of 1 orange
sugar-free sweetener to taste

Heat the oven to 180°C/350°F/gas 4.

Split the bananas in half lengthways and arrange in an oven-proof dish. Mix the juices, rum and cinnamon together and pour over the bananas. Scatter the orange rind over the bananas and bake for 20 minutes, basting occasionally. Five minutes before removing from the oven, mix the sweetener with some of the basting liquid and spoon over the bananas. Serve hot or cold.

A Cream Substitute from page 89 may be served with the bananas.

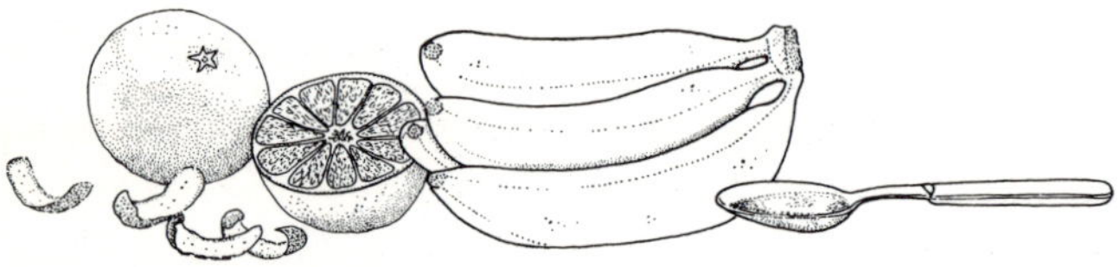

Rum, raisin and pineapple yoghurt

Serves 4

Each serving: 120 kcal/500 kJ, 20 g (2 units) carbohydrate, 5 g fibre, 5 g protein, 1 g fat

300 ml/½ pt low-fat plain yoghurt
300 g/10½ oz crushed pineapple, canned without sugar
1 tbsp rum, or rum flavouring to taste
50 g/1⅔ oz chopped raisins
4 tbsp natural bran flakes
sugar-free sweetener to taste
yellow food colouring
pinch grated nutmeg

Mix all the ingredients together, place in glass goblets and chill. Just before serving, grate a little fresh nutmeg over the top.

Raspberry yoghurt pudding

Serves 4

Each serving: 50 kcal/210 kJ, 10 g (1 unit) carbohydrate, 8 g fibre, 4 g protein, negligible fat

*450 g/1 lb fresh or frozen raspberries**
sugar-free sweetener equivalent to 60 g/4 tbsp sugar
150 ml/¼ pt low-fat plain yoghurt, chilled
1 egg white, stiffly beaten

Heat half the raspberries gently for a few minutes until the juice starts to flow and the fruit starts to break down. Crush and sweeten. When cold, stir in the yoghurt, then the egg white. Decorate with the remaining raspberries and serve at once

Spiced oranges

Serves 4

Each serving: 60 kcal/250 kJ, 10 g (1 unit) carbohydrate, 2 g fibre, 1 g protein, 0 g fat

4 medium-sized oranges, peeled and free of pith
small stick cinnamon
2 cloves
pinch grated nutmeg
4 tbsp sugar-free orange squash
2 tbsp brandy
sugar-free sweetener to taste

Slice the oranges very thinly, then quarter the slices and put into a basin along with any juice. Put the cinnamon stick and cloves in a small saucepan with about 150 ml/¼ pt cold water. Bring to simmering point and simmer for about 5 minutes. Add a large pinch of grated nutmeg and leave to cool. Remove the cinnamon and cloves and add the orange squash, brandy, and sweetener. Pour over the oranges and allow to marinate in a cool place for an hour before serving in individual glasses.

Gooseberry fool

Serves 4

Each serving: 50 kcal/210 kJ, negligible (0 units) carbohydrate, 3 g fibre, 6 g protein, 1 g fat

400 g/14 oz gooseberries, cooked†
100 g/3½ oz low-fat plain yoghurt
100 g/3½ oz skimmed milk curd cheese
sugar-free sweetener to taste
few drops green food colouring

➧

*Loganberries may be used instead.

† Other fruits, such as rhubarb or blackcurrants, may be used.

Purée the fruit in a blender. Stir the yoghurt into the cheese, then pour into the blender with the machine running until they are just mixed. Add the sweetener and colouring, and mix in. Spoon into tall glasses and chill for an hour before serving.

Loganberry cheesecake

See page 82

Serves 6

Each serving: 180 kcal/760 kJ, 10 g (1 unit) carbohydrate, 7 g fibre, 15 g protein, 8 g fat

100 g/3½ oz wholemeal bread, crumbed
2 tbsp natural bran flakes
1 tsp ground cinnamon
4 tbsp low-fat margarine (spread)
2 tsp gelatine dissolved in 2 tbsp hot water
500 g/17½ oz skimmed milk curd cheese
grated rind of 1 lemon
sugar-free liquid sweetener to taste
450 g/1 lb fresh loganberries, stewed, or canned in natural juice
6 tbsp loganberry juice
2 tsp arrowroot

Toast the breadcrumbs and mix with the bran, cinnamon and low-fat margarine. Press into the base of a medium-sized flan tin and leave to cool. Beat the dissolved gelatine into the cheese and add the lemon rind and sweetener. Spread over the prepared base and chill.

Place the loganberries and juice in a saucepan, mix the arrowroot to a paste with a little cold juice and add to the loganberries. Bring to the boil, stirring constantly until thickened. Cool and spread over the filling. Chill slightly before serving.

Fromage blanc and fruit

See page 82

Serves 6

Each serving: 100 kcal/420 kJ, 10 g (1 unit) carbohydrate, 9 g fibre, 8 g protein, 2 g fat

6 tbsp coarse oatmeal
sugar-free sweetener to taste
250 g/9 oz fromage blanc or Cream Substitute II (see page 89)*
680 g/1½ lb fresh or frozen raspberries or other soft fruit

Toast the oatmeal lightly under a slow grill and set aside to cool. Add sweetener to the fromage blanc, then gently stir in the toasted oatmeal and half the raspberries. Put a spoonful of the remaining raspberries into each of the 6 tall glasses, then half the fromage blanc mixture followed by another spoonful of raspberries. Fill up with the remaining fromage blanc mixture and decorate the top with the rest of the raspberries. Serve well chilled.

---

*Other skimmed milk curd cheese may be used.

Summer fruit salad

Serves 6

Each serving: 40 kcal/170 kJ, 10 g (1 unit) carbohydrate, 7 g fibre, 1 g protein, 0 g fat

100 ml/3½ fl oz fresh orange juice
3 tbsp brandy or pure kirsch (optional)
400 ml/14 fl oz sugar-free sparkling drink
sugar-free sweetener to taste
160 g/5½ oz strawberries
180 g/6½ oz raspberries
100 g/3½ oz red currants
60 g/2 oz white currants
100 g/3½ oz black, red or mixed dessert cherries
100 g/3½ oz blackberries

Mix together the liquid ingredients. Prepare the fruit by removing hulls and stones, and slicing larger pieces of fruit but leaving small fruit whole. As the fruit is prepared, put it into the orange liquid. Leave to soak for 3–4 hours. Then serve with home-made Sorbet (see pages 88–9).

Apricot snow

Serves 4

Each serving: 80 kcal/340 kJ, 10 g (1 unit) carbohydrate, 6 g fibre, 5 g protein, 1 g fat

250 g/9 oz stewed dried apricots
2 tsp gelatine dissolved in 4 tbsp hot water
2 egg whites, stiffly whipped
few drops almond essence (optional)
1 tbsp chopped almonds, toasted

Purée the apricots in a blender. Add the dissolved gelatine to the purée. Fold the beaten egg whites and almond essence, if used, into the purée and pour into a serving dish, or individual dishes. Sprinkle with chopped almonds before serving.

Blackberry and apple crunchie

Serves 4

Each serving: 70 kcal/290 kJ, 10 g (1 unit) carbohydrate, 5 g fibre, 4 g protein, negligible fat

150 ml/¼ pt low-fat plain yoghurt
sugar-free sweetener to taste
200 g/7 oz skimmed milk curd cheese
200 g /7 oz blackberries
2 medium-sized red apples, cored and diced
sprigs of mint

Stir the yoghurt and sweetener into the cheese. Reserve 4 blackberries for decoration, then add the remainder with the apples to the cheese mixture. Serve, slightly chilled, in individual dishes decorated with the reserved blackberries and mint.

Blackcurrant charlotte

See page 82

Serves 4

Each serving: 130 kcal/550 kJ, 20 g (2 units) carbohydrate, 13 g fibre, 4 g protein, 4 g fat

450 g/1 lb blackcurrants
140 g/5 oz wholemeal breadcrumbs
2 tbsp lemon juice
sugar-free sweetener to taste
few tbsp water
1 tbsp polyunsaturated margarine

Heat the oven to 190°C/375°F/gas 5.

Place a layer of blackcurrants in a small, deep, non-stick pie dish and sprinkle a layer of breadcrumbs on top. Repeat these layers, finishing with a layer of breadcrumbs, but before the final layer, pour over the lemon juice mixed with the sweetener and a few tablespoons of water. Dot the final layer with the margarine. Bake for 30–35 minutes or until the top is crisp and lightly browned. Serve hot.

Lemon sorbet

Serves 4

Used in small quantities this recipe need not be included in daily calculations.

finely grated rind of 1 lemon
300 ml/½ pt water
2 tsp gelatine soaked in 2 tbsp cold water
5 tbsp lemon juice
sugar-free sweetener equivalent to 75 g/5 tbsp sugar, or to taste
1 egg white, lightly beaten

Bring the lemon rind and water to the boil, then allow to cool a little. Add the soaked gelatine and stir until it dissolves. Cool, and mix in the lemon juice, sweetener and egg white. Freeze until it begins to set round the edges. Turn out into a cold basin and whisk until it is thick and white. Return to the freezing compartment and freeze until firm. Allow to soften slightly in the main compartment of the refrigerator for ½–1 hour before serving. Spoon into serving glasses or use in place of cream on cold sweets.

Orange sorbet

Serves 4

Used in small quantities this recipe need not be included in daily calculations

finely grated rind of 2 oranges
240 ml/ 8 fl oz water
2 tsp gelatine soaked in 2 tbsp cold water
juice of 2 medium-sized oranges
sugar-free sweetener equivalent to 75 g/5 tbsp sugar, or to taste
1 egg white, lightly beaten

Make and use as for Lemon Sorbet above.

Raspberry sorbet

Serves 6

Each serving: 30 kcal/130 kJ, 5 g (½ unit) carbohydrate, 6 g fibre, 3 g protein, 0 g fat

450 g/1 lb fresh or frozen raspberries
4 tbsp orange juice
sugar-free sweetener equivalent to 60 g/4 tbsp sugar, or to taste
2 tsp gelatine dissolved in 2 tbsp hot water
1 egg white, stiffly beaten

Purée the raspberries in a blender. Mix in the orange juice, sweetener and the dissolved gelatine. Freeze until half frozen. Empty into a cold bowl and beat until smooth, then fold in the egg white. Finish freezing as in Lemon Sorbet opposite.

Strawberry sorbet

Serves 6

Each serving: 30 kcal/130 kJ, 5 g (½ unit) carbohydrate, 2 g fibre, 3 g protein, 0 g fat

Make as for Raspberry Sorbet above, using strawberries.

Cream substitute I

Each 30 ml/2 tbsp: 20 kcal/80 kJ, negligible (0 units) carbohydrate, 0 g fibre, 1 g protein, 1 g fat

100 ml/3½ fl oz well-chilled evaporated milk
sugar-free sweetener to taste
flavouring to taste

Whip the chilled milk until it is smooth and thick, and has trebled in volume. Add sweetener and flavouring. This can be kept for a few days in the refrigerator.

Cream substitute II

Each 30 ml/2 tbsp: 20 kcal/80 kJ, negligible (0 units) carbohydrate, 0 g fibre, 2 g protein, 1 g fat

150 ml/¼ pt low-fat plain yoghurt
120 g/4¼ oz low-fat plain cottage cheese
1½ tbsp lemon juice or mixture of lemon juice and orange juice
sugar-free sweetener to taste
flavouring to taste

Purée the ingredients in a blender until smooth and resembling the texture of lightly whipped cream. This can be kept for a few days in the refrigerator.

BAKING

Sweet or savoury flan case

Serves 4

Each serving: 140 kcal/590 kJ, 20 g (2 units) carbohydrate, 3 g fibre, 3 g protein, 7 g fat

100 g /3½ oz wholemeal flour
1 tsp baking powder (optional)
¼ tsp salt
30 g/1 oz polyunsaturated margarine
50 g/1⅔ oz mashed potatoes
cold water to mix, if necessary

Heat the oven to 200°C/400°F/gas 6.

Mix the flour, baking powder, if used, and salt together and rub in the margarine until the mixture resembles fine breadcrumbs. Knead with the mashed potato and water, if used, until a stiff dough is formed. Roll to the required size between sheets of greaseproof paper. Peel off the top sheet of paper, lift the dough, still on the bottom layer of paper, and invert to line an 18–20 cm/7–8 in flan dish. Remove the paper. Prick the base and bake blind for 20–25 minutes.

For a savoury flan case, flavoured salt can be substituted for ordinary salt and ¼ tsp dried mustard or about 1 tbsp finely chopped fresh herbs added.

Strawberry flan

Serves 6

Each serving: 160 kcal/670 kJ, 20 g (2 units) carbohydrate, 4 g fibre, 7 g protein, 6 g fat

2 tbsp brandy or pure kirsch
500 g/18 oz fresh or frozen strawberries
sugar-free sweetener equivalent to 45 g/3 tbsp sugar
200 g/7 oz skimmed milk curd cheese
20 cm/8 in flan case, baked blind (see above)

Sprinkle the brandy or kirsch over the prepared strawberries and marinate in the refrigerator, turning occasionally, for at least 30 minutes. Just before serving, add the sweetener and the liquor from the strawberries to the cheese and beat well with a fork. Spread over the base of the cold flan case and place the strawberries, rounded side up, evenly on top of the cheese mixture. Serve.

Hunz Bunz (top, see p. 94), Bran Popovers with Dates (centre, see p. 97), Buttermilk Scones (bottom, see p. 97).

Raspberry flan

Serves 6
Each serving: 160 kcal/670 kJ, 20 g (2 units) carbohydrate, 8 g fibre, 7 g protein, 6 g fat

Make as Strawberry Flan on page 90, spooning 500 g/18 oz raspberries over the cheese filling just before serving.

Raisin and oatmeal bread

Makes 30 slices
Each slice: 60 kcal/250 kJ, 10 g (1 unit) carbohydrate, 2 g fibre, 3 g protein, 1 g fat

340 g/12 oz wholemeal self-raising flour
115 g/4 oz medium oatmeal
1 tsp salt
100 g/3½ oz raisins, chopped
2–3 tsp mixed spice (optional)
sugar-free sweetener equivalent to 30 g/2 tbsp sugar
300 ml/½ pt low-fat plain yoghurt
2–4 tbsp water

Heat the oven to 200°C/400°F/gas 6.

Mix all the dry ingredients together. Add the sweetener to the yoghurt and water, stir into the dry ingredients and mix to a light elastic dough. Shape to fit a 450 g/1 lb non-stick loaf tin. Bake for 40–45 minutes or until well risen and golden brown. Cool on a wire tray.

Country squares

Makes 25
Each square: 90 kcal/380 kJ, 10 g (1 unit) carbohydrate, 4 g fibre, 2 g protein, 4 g fat

200 g/7 oz wholemeal flour
2 tsp baking powder
pinch salt
100 g/3½ oz polyunsaturated margarine
sugar-free liquid sweetener equivalent to 60 g/4 tbsp sugar
70 g/2½ oz mashed potatoes (or instant mashed potato)
100 g/3½ oz carrots, finely grated
100 g/3½ oz cooking apples, grated
6 tbsp large-flake natural bran
100 g/3½ oz dried apricots, chopped
100 g/3½ oz dried prunes, chopped
60 g/2 oz seedless raisins, chopped
½ tsp grated nutmeg
½ tsp ground cinnamon
2 eggs, beaten

Heat the oven to 180°C/350°F/gas 4.

Mix the flour, baking powder and salt together and rub in the margarine until the mixture resembles fine breadcrumbs. Knead

---

Rasin and Oatmeal Bread (top), Oatmeal Fingers (centre, see p. 96), Country Squares (bottom).

the sweetener into the potatoes and add to the flour mixture with the carrots, apples, bran, dried fruit and spices. Beat in the eggs to form a fairly stiff dough. Spread into a 23–25 cm/9–10 in non-stick square shallow tin and bake for 30–35 minutes. Leave to cool, then cut into squares.

Hunz bunz

See page 91

Makes 24

Each bun: 80 kcal/340 kJ, 10 g (1 unit) carbohydrate, 2 g fibre, 2 g protein, 3 g fat

200 g/7 oz wholemeal flour
60 g/2 oz millet flakes, or 60 g/2 oz extra flour
3 tsp baking powder
pinch salt
60 g/2 oz polyunsaturated margarine
sugar-free liquid sweetener equivalent to 90 g/6 tbsp sugar
100 g/3½ oz mashed potatoes (or instant mashed potato)
1 tsp almond essence
100 g/3½ oz dried apricots, chopped
1 egg, beaten
2 tbsp low-fat plain yoghurt
30 g/1 oz flaked almonds
1 tsp polyunsaturated margarine (to grease)

Heat the oven to 200°C/400°F/gas 6.

Mix the flour, millet flakes, baking powder and salt together and rub in the margarine until the mixture resembles fine breadcrumbs. Knead the sweetener into the potatoes and add to the flour mixture with the almond essence and apricots. Beat in the egg and yoghurt to form a stiff dough. Spoon the mixture into small rough heaps in a shallow greased tin and put a piece of flaked almond on top of each heap. Bake for about 15 minutes. Cool on a wire tray.

Banana and bran buns

Makes 16

Each bun: 70 kcal/290 kJ, 10 g (1 unit) carbohydrate, 3 g fibre, 2 g protein, 2 g fat

150 g/5 oz wholemeal self-raising flour
50 g/1⅔ oz natural bran flakes
½ tsp salt
2 tbsp polyunsaturated margarine
1 egg, beaten
250 g/9 oz peeled banana, well mashed
grated rind of 1 lemon or orange
sugar-free sweetener equivalent to 90 g/6 tbsp sugar

Heat the oven to 190°C/375°F/gas 5.

Mix the flour, bran and salt together and rub in the margarine until the mixture resembles fine breadcrumbs. Mix the egg, banana, rind and sweetener together (or put through a blender) and beat into the flour until a smooth dough is formed. Spoon into 16 non-stick patty tins and bake for about 15 minutes, or until the buns are risen and brown.

Fruit tea bread

Makes 12 slices

Each slice: 100 kcal/420 kJ, 20 g (2 units) carbohydrate, 3 g fibre, 3 g protein, 1 g fat

150 ml/¼ pt hot tea
200 g/7 oz mixed dried fruit (calculated as 100 g/3½ oz sultanas, 100 g/3½ oz seedless raisins)
5 tbsp orange juice
sugar-free sweetener equivalent to 90 g/6 tbsp sugar
1 egg, beaten
200 g/7 oz self-raising wholemeal flour
¼ tsp mixed spice

Heat the oven to 180°C/350°F/gas 4.

Pour the tea over the fruit, cover and soak overnight then discard any unabsorbed tea. Add the fruit juice and sweetener to the egg and mix into the fruit. Mix the flour and spice together and stir into the fruit mixture. Turn into a 450 g/1 lb non-stick loaf tin and bake for 45 minutes. Cool on a wire tray.

Wholemeal orange biscuits

Makes 30

Each biscuit: 50 kcal/210 kJ, 5 g (½ unit) carbohydrate, 2 g fibre, 2 g protein, 2 g fat

200 g/7 oz wholemeal flour
70 g/2½ oz large-flake natural bran
2 tsp baking powder
finely grated rind of 1 orange
¼ tsp salt
1 tsp mixed spice
60 g/2 oz polyunsaturated margarine
70 g/2½ oz mashed potatoes (or instant mashed potato)
sugar-free liquid sweetener equivalent to 60 g/4 tbsp sugar
1 egg, beaten
3 tbsp orange juice
1 tsp polyunsaturated margarine (to grease)

Heat the oven to 180°C/350°F/gas 4.

Mix the flour, bran, baking powder, orange rind, salt and spice together and rub in the margarine until the mixture resembles fine breadcrumbs. Knead the sweetener into the potatoes and add the flour mixture. Beat in the egg and orange juice to form a stiff dough. Roll out thinly on a floured board and cut into squares or rounds using a 5 cm/2 in cutter. Place on greased baking trays and bake for 15–20 minutes or until crisp but not brown. Cool on a wire tray and store in an airtight container.

Savoury biscuits
Make as Wholemeal Orange Biscuits above, but omit the sweetener, spice, orange and salt and add 1 tsp Marmite or other yeast-and-vegetable extract, ½ tsp celery salt, 1 tbsp grated onion and a good pinch of cayenne pepper.

Oatmeal fingers

See page 92

Makes 24
Each finger: 50 kcal/210 kJ, 5 g (½ unit) carbohydrate, 2 g fibre, 2 g protein, 3 g fat

60 g/2 oz medium oatmeal
100 g/3½ oz wholemeal self-raising flour
60 g/2 oz natural bran flakes
¼ tsp salt
½ tsp grated nutmeg, cloves, ground cinnamon, and mixed spice, or to taste
60 g/2 oz polyunsaturated margarine
sugar-free sweetener equivalent to 60 g/4 tbsp sugar
1 egg, beaten
2 tbsp orange juice
1 tsp polyunsaturated margarine (to grease)

Heat the oven to 180°C/350°F/gas 4.

Mix the oatmeal, flour, bran, salt and spices together and rub in the margarine until the mixture resembles fine breadcrumbs. Stir the sweetener into the mixed egg and orange juice, and beat into the flour mixture. Knead together and roll out thinly on a floured board. Cut into 5 cm/2 in fingers and place on greased trays. Bake for 15–20 minutes or until crisp and lightly browned. Cool on a rack and store in an airtight container.

Bran popovers

Makes 12
Each popover: 70 kcal/290 kJ, 10 g (1 unit) carbohydrate, 4 g fibre, 4 g protein, 2 g fat

115 g/4 oz wholemeal flour
2 tsp baking powder
½ tsp salt
85 g/3 oz natural bran flakes
sugar-free sweetener equivalent to 45 g/3 tbsp sugar
1 egg, beaten
300 ml/½ pt skimmed milk
1 tbsp polyunsaturated oil

Heat the oven to 200°C/400°F/gas 6.

Place the dry ingredients in a bowl. Add the sweetener to the egg, milk and oil and beat together. Mix into the dry ingredients.

Divide the mixture between 12 non-stick patty tins and bake for 25–30 minutes. Serve hot, cold or toasted for breakfast, or for a small snack at any time of the day.

For variety add 2 tsp spice or 1–2 tsp grated orange rind or 1 small carrot, grated. They may be spread with quark, curd cheese or sugar-free marmalade.

Popovers with dates

See page 91

Each popover: 80 kcal/350 kJ, 10 g (1 unit) carbohydrate, 5 g fibre, 4 g protein, 2 g fat.

60 g/2 oz dates, chopped
1 tsp grated lemon or orange rind (optional)

Add the chopped dates to the dry ingredients and continue as Bran Popovers above.

Popovers with apricots

Each popover: 80 kcal/350 kJ, 10 g (1 unit) carbohydrate, 5 g fibre, 4 g protein, 2 g fat

60 g/2 oz dried apricots, chopped

Add the chopped apricots to the dry ingredients and continue as Bran Popovers above.

Buttermilk scones

See page 91

Makes 12

Each scone: 80 kcal/340 kJ, 10 g (1 unit) carbohydrate, 3 g fibre, 3 g protein, 3 g fat

200 g/7 oz wholemeal flour
4 tbsp natural bran flakes
1 tsp bicarbonate of soda
1 tsp cream of tartar
½ tsp salt
30 g/1 oz polyunsaturated margarine
sugar-free sweetener equivalent to 30 g/2 tbsp sugar
150 ml/¼ pt buttermilk or soured skimmed milk, or use fresh skimmed milk and 1 extra tsp cream of tartar

Heat the oven to 220°C/425°F/gas 7.

Mix the dry ingredients together and rub in the margarine until the mixture resembles fine breadcrumbs. Add the sweetener to the milk and stir into the flour to form a soft dough. Roll out lightly on a floured board to 12 mm/½ in thick and cut into rounds using a 5 cm/2 in cutter. Place on a non-stick baking tray, brush with a little milk and bake for 8–10 minutes. Cool on a wire tray.

➧

Fruit scones
Add 30 g/1 oz raisins or sultanas, chopped, to the rubbed-in mixture.

Date scones
Add 45 g/1½ oz dates, chopped, to the rubbed-in mixture.

Biscuits with sesame seeds

Makes 16

Each biscuit: 50 kcal/210 kJ, 5 g (½ unit) carbohydrate, 1 g fibre, 1 g protein, 3 g fat

100 g/3½ oz wholemeal self-raising flour
pinch salt
½ tsp mixed spice
45 g/1½ oz polyunsaturated margarine
sugar-free sweetener equivalent to 60 g/4 tbsp sugar
1 egg, beaten
2 tbsp sesame seeds
1 tsp margarine (to grease)

Heat the oven to 180°C/350°F/gas 4.

Mix the flour, salt and spice together and rub in the margarine until the mixture resembles fine breadcrumbs. Add the sweetener to the egg and stir into the flour mixture to form a stiff dough. Knead well and roll out thinly on to a floured board. Brush with a little cold water, sprinkle over the sesame seeds and press lightly into the mixture. Cut into 16 equal-sized squares or oblongs and place on a greased baking tray. Bake for 15–20 minutes or until crisp. Cool on a wire tray and store in an airtight container.

SAUCES AND DRESSINGS

SAUCES

Barbecue sauce

Serves 6

Each serving: 10 kcal/40 kJ, negligible (0 units) carbohydrate, 1 g fibre, negligible protein, 0 g fat

225 g/8 oz canned tomatoes, chopped with juice
2 medium-sized onions, chopped
½ tsp dried basil
1 clove garlic, crushed
seasoning

Put all the ingredients into a saucepan and simmer together until thick and pulpy. Purée in a blender and adjust the seasoning before serving.

Spicy barbecue sauce

Serves 10

Each serving: 20 kcal/80 kJ, negligible (0 units) carbohydrate, negligible fibre, negligible protein, 1 g fat

1 tbsp polyunsaturated oil
600 ml/1 pt beef stock
2 medium-sized onions, chopped
1 clove garlic, crushed
1 medium-sized red pepper, chopped
½ tsp chilli powder, or to taste
few drops tabasco sauce
2 tsp Worcester sauce
grated rind of 1 lemon
sugar-free sweetener to taste

Heat the oil and a few spoonfuls of stock and fry the onions, garlic and pepper gently for 5 minutes, until transparent. Add all the remaining ingredients, except the sweetener and bring to the boil. Cover and simmer for 20 minutes. Remove from the heat and stir in the sweetener before serving.

Thin pouring sauce

Serves 4

Each serving: 50 kcal/210 kJ, 5 g (½ unit) carbohydrate, negligible fibre, 3 g protein, 2 g fat

250 ml/9 fl oz skimmed milk
2 tsp polyunsaturated oil or margarine
1½ tbsp wholemeal flour
seasoning

Put the milk and oil into a saucepan and gradually whisk in the flour. Heat gently until the mixture thickens and boils, whisking constantly. Cook for 3 minutes, then season.

Variations

Anchovy sauce Add 1–2 tsp anchovy essence.

Caper sauce Add 2 tbsp roughly chopped capers and, if liked, 1 tsp caper vinegar.

Parsley sauce Add 2–3 tbsp freshly chopped parsley and, if liked, 1 tsp lemon juice.

Onion sauce Add 150 g/5 oz onion, boiled, drained and chopped and ¼ tsp onion or garlic salt.

Sweet and sour sauce

See page 51

Serves 4

Each serving: 30 kcal/130 kJ, 5 g (½ unit) carbohydrate, 1 g fibre, 1 g protein, negligible fat

1 small onion, chopped
3 pineappple rings, canned in natural juice, cubed
45 g/1½ oz cooked haricot or other white beans (see pages 12–13)
2 tbsp vinegar
2 tsp soya sauce
2 tsp tomato purée or ketchup
pinch salt
300 ml/½ pt natural pineapple juice from the can made up with water if necessary
sugar-free sweetener to taste
60 g/2 oz mustard pickles (optional, for very spicy flavour)

Purée the onion, pineapple cubes and beans in a blender. Add the remaining ingredients and blend together until smooth. Serve with pork or chicken.

Wine and mushroom sauce

Serves 4

Each serving: 80 kcal/340 kJ, 5 g (½ unit) carbohydrate, 2 g fibre, 2 g protein, 3 g fat

1 tbsp polyunsaturated margarine
1 medium-sized onion, finely chopped
200 g/7 oz mushrooms, finely chopped
300 ml/½ pt chicken stock
150 ml/¼ pt dry red wine
1 tbsp Worcester sauce
15 g/½ oz potato or wholemeal flour
seasoning

Melt the margarine in a saucepan. Add the onion and fry gently until soft, stirring occasionally. Add the mushrooms and cook over low heat for 2 minutes, stirring. Add the stock, wine and Worcester sauce and simmer for 10 minutes.

Blend the flour with a little water, stir into the mixture and return to the boil. Add the sweetener and seasoning and simmer for a further 5 minutes or until thickened. Serve with meats or use as a basis for reheating meats, beans or other foods.

Tomato sauce

Serves 4

Each serving: 50 kcal/210 kJ, negligible (0 units) carbohydrate, 1 g fibre, 1 g protein, 4 g fat

1 tbsp polyunsaturated oil
1 medium-sized onion, finely chopped
5 tbsp tomato purée
pinch thyme
300 ml/½ pt water
seasoning

Heat the oil in a saucepan. Add the onion and fry gently for 5 minutes until transparent. Add the tomato purée and cook for a few minutes, stirring. Stir in the thyme and water, cover and simmer gently for 25–30 minutes. Season to taste before serving.

Tomato chutney

Used in small amounts this does not need to be counted in daily calculations

900 g/2 lb green tomatoes, roughly chopped
1 large onion, chopped
1 large cooking apple, peeled and chopped
1 clove garlic, crushed (optional)
300 ml/½ pt white or malt vinegar
1–2 tsp mixed pickling spices (tied in muslin)
60 g/2 oz raisins or sultanas, chopped
½ tsp salt
sugar-free liquid sweetener equivalent to 285 g/10 oz sugar

Put the vegetables and fresh fruit into a saucepan with about half the vinegar and the spices. Simmer gently until they start to become soft. Add the remainder of the vinegar gradually, then add the remaining ingredients and cook until soft and pulpy. Remove the spices and while still hot, pour into warmed jars to within 12 cm/½ in of the top. Cover carefully with several thicknesses of waxed or greaseproof paper (to prevent the chutney from coming into contact with metal lids) or use purpose-made discs and treated plastic tops.

DRESSINGS

Lowest in fat and simple to make are seasoned yoghurt dressings. Used in small quantities they do not have to be included in your daily calculations. To make, stir all the ingredients into the yoghurt and mix well.

Basic yoghurt dressing

150 ml/¼ pt low-fat plain yoghurt
1 tbsp lemon juice
½ tsp prepared mustard
¼ tsp salt
pepper

Additions

Add one or more of the following: finely chopped onions, cucumber or peppers; ½–1 clove garlic, crushed; garlic, onion or celery salt in place of plain salt; 2–3 drops tabasco sauce; 1 tbsp tomato ketchup (sugar-free) or chilli sauce; sugar-free proprietary salad seasonings and mixes.

Curry dressing

150 ml/¼ pt low-fat plain yoghurt
1 tbsp lemon juice
1 tbsp chopped unsweetened pickle
¼ tsp salt
pepper
2–3 drops sugar-free liquid sweetener
2 tsp curry powder
other curry spices, if liked

Piquant dressing

150 ml/¼ pt low-fat yoghurt
½ tsp prepared mustard
¼ tsp garlic salt
2 tsp Worcester sauce
2–3 drops tabasco sauce

Green dressing

150 ml/¼ pt low-fat plain yoghurt
¼ tsp garlic salt
½ tsp prepared mustard
2 tbsp finely chopped onion
2 tbsp chopped gherkins
2 tbsp chopped capers or other sugar-free green pickles
4 tbsp chopped parsley or mixture of parsley and other green herbs, the type depending on the dish it is to accompany
1 tbsp lemon juice, or vinegar from jar of pickles

Add all the ingredients to the yoghurt and mix. Alternatively, put all the ingredients (unchopped) into a blender and purée to a smooth consistency. Use as a dressing or sauce with fish, chicken and cold meats.

SNACKS

Havana rice and black beans

See page 110

Serves 4

Each serving: 330 kcal/1390 kJ, 50 g (5 units) carbohydrate, 13 g fibre, 12 g protein, 5 g fat

115 g/4 oz long-grain brown rice
1 tbsp polyunsaturated oil
1 small onion, chopped
1 small green pepper, chopped
1 clove garlic, crushed
4 tbsp dry red wine
seasoning
1 small bay leaf
600 g/1 lb 5 oz cooked black beans, hot (see pages 12–13)

While the rice is cooking (see page 14), heat the oil in a saucepan. Add the onion, pepper and garlic and fry gently until the onion is golden brown. Add the wine, seasoning and bay leaf and continue to cook gently for a further 10 minutes. Stir in the hot beans, cover and cook over a moderate heat for a further 20 minutes. Spoon the beans into the centre of a hot serving dish and surround with the newly cooked rice. This dish may be garnished with peppers and parsley.

Red beans and rice

Serves 4

Each serving: 300 kcal/1260 kJ, 50 g (5 units) carbohydrate, 11 g fibre, 13 g protein, 7 g fat

1 tbsp polyunsaturated oil
150 ml/¼ pt stock
2 medium-sized onions, finely chopped
1 medium-sized carrot, finely chopped
1 clove garlic, crushed
2 stalks celery, chopped
300 g/10½ oz canned tomatoes, chopped with juice
pinch dried thyme and rosemary
few blades of rosemary
2 tbsp chopped parsley
seasoning
400 g/14 oz cooked red kidney beans (see pages 12–13)
300 g/10½ oz cooked long-grain brown rice (see page 14)
3 tbsp grated Parmesan cheese or other strong cheese

Heat the oil with a few spoonfuls of stock, add the fresh vegetables and cover, allowing them to cook gently in their own juice for 10 minutes. Stir occasionally. Add the tomatoes, the remaining stock, the herbs and seasoning along with the beans and rice. Stir well, bring to the boil and simmer for 15–20 minutes or until all the vegetables are cooked. Sprinkle the cheese over the top before serving.

Soya beans in spicy barbecue sauce

Serves 4

Each serving: 220 kcal/920 kJ, 20 g (2 units) carbohydrate, 6 g fibre, 17 g protein, 10 g fat

600 g/1 lb 5 oz cooked soya beans (see pages 12–13)
½ quantity Spicy Barbecue Sauce (see page 99)

Add the soya beans to the sauce. Bring to the boil, then simmer for 10–20 minutes. Serve with vegetables or, for a snack, serve on wholemeal toast.

Note

Other beans can be used in a similar way – for example chick peas in Sweet and Sour Sauce or cannellini beans in Wine and Mushroom Sauce (see page 100).

Curried soya beans

Serves 4

Each serving: 240 kcal/1010 kJ, 30 g (3 units) carbohydrate, 9 g fibre, 17 g protein, 8 g fat

600 g/1 lb 5 oz cooked soya beans (see pages 12–13)
2 medium-sized onions, chopped
1 clove garlic, crushed
2 medium-sized cooking apples, cored and diced
2 medium-sized tomatoes, chopped
2 tsp curry powder, or to taste
1 tsp curry paste
250 ml/9 fl oz chicken stock
½ tsp salt
¼ tsp pepper
2 tsp lemon juice
few drops sugar-free liquid sweetener

Put the beans with all the other ingredients, except the sweetener, into a heavy-based saucepan. Bring to the boil, cover and simmer until the apples and onions are tender. Stir in the sweetener and serve with plainly cooked long-grain brown rice (see page 14).

Savoury spaghetti with chick peas

Serves 4

See page 109

Each serving: 380 kcal/1600 kJ, 60 g (6 units) carbohydrate, 16 g fibre, 19 g protein, 8 g fat

1 tbsp polyunsaturated oil
1 medium-sized onion, chopped
1 clove garlic, crushed
60 g/2 oz lean ham, chopped
4 medium-sized tomatoes, chopped
½ tsp dried mixed herbs
½ tsp celery salt
pepper
300 g/10½ oz chick peas canned without sugar, or cooked chick peas (see pages 12–13)
250 g/9 oz wholemeal spaghetti

Heat the oil. Add the onion and garlic and fry gently for 5 minutes until transparent. Add the ham, tomatoes, herbs and seasoning, cover and simmer for about 10 minutes. Stir in the chick peas and heat through.

Meanwhile, cook the spaghetti in boiling salted water (see page 15). Drain, mix with the vegetables and serve.

Sausage risotto

Serves 4

Each serving: 310 kcal/1300 kJ, 40 g (4 units) carbohydrate, 9 g fibre, 10 g protein, 12 g fat

2 tsp polyunsaturated oil
3 tbsp meat stock
4 chipolata sausages, grilled and thinly sliced
1 large onion, chopped
100 g/3½ oz button mushrooms, sliced
4 medium-sized tomatoes, quartered
200 g/7 oz canned processed peas, drained
350 g/12½ oz cooked long-grain brown rice (see page 14), hot
1 tbsp tomato ketchup
1 tbsp Worcester sauce, or to taste
seasoning
1 large tomato, quartered
parsley

Heat the oil with the stock and fry the sausage slices for 2–3 minutes. Add the onion and cook gently until transparent. Stir in the mushrooms and tomatoes and continue to cook for 5 minutes. Add the peas, rice, ketchup and Worcester sauce, adding a little extra stock if necessary, and cook until heated through, stirring. Adjust the seasoning if necessary, then turn on to a hot serving dish. Garnish with tomato quarters and parsley before serving.

Tuna and anchovy quiche

See page 110

Serves 4

Each serving: 300 kcal/1260 kJ, 30 g (3 units) carbohydrate, 6 g fibre, 17 g protein, 12 g fat

20 cm/8 in flan case, baked blind (see page 90)
1 small onion, chopped
200 g/7 oz sweetcorn kernels
100 g/3½ oz mushrooms, sliced
1 tbsp lemon juice
100 g/3½ oz canned tuna fish in brine, drained and flaked
60 g/2 oz canned anchovies, drained and chopped
½ tsp garlic salt
pepper
1 egg
150 ml/¼ pt skimmed milk
3 small tomatoes, quartered
few sprigs of parsley

Heat the oven to 200°C/400°F/gas 6.

Arrange the vegetables, lemon juice, fish and light seasoning in the flan case. Beat the egg, add it to the milk and pour over the fish mixture. Return the flan case to the oven and bake for 45–50 minutes or until the filling has set.

Garnish with tomatoes and parsley. Serve hot or cold.

Chicken liver savoury

Serves 4

Each serving: 190 kcal/800 kJ, 10 g (1 unit) carbohydrate, 5 g fibre, 17 g protein, 8 g fat

1 tbsp polyunsaturated margarine
4 tbsp stock
200 g/7 oz chicken livers, cut into neat pieces
60 g /2 oz lean ham slices, cut into short strips
4 medium-sized tomatoes, chopped
225 g/8 oz mushrooms, sliced
1 tsp chopped basil or ½ tsp dried basil
seasoning
115 g/4 oz sliced wholemeal bread, toasted

Melt the margarine with the stock or boiling water and cook the livers gently until they lose their pinkness. Add the ham and tomatoes and cook for a further 5 minutes, stirring occasionally. Stir in the mushrooms, basil and seasoning, and cook for a further few minutes until all the ingredients are heated through. Serve on wholemeal toast.

Savoury beef pasties

Makes 3

Each pasty: 280 kcal/1180 kJ, 30 g (3 units) carbohydrate, 6g fibre, 16 g protein, 12 g fat

100 g/3½ oz wholemeal flour as pastry (see page 90)
1 tsp polyunsaturated margarine
2 tbsp chopped onions
1 medium-sized carrot, grated
2 tbsp stock or water
2 tbsp cooked haricot or other beans (see pages 12–13)
½ tsp low-calorie tomato ketchup
½ tsp Worcester sauce
100 g/3½ oz cooked lean beef, chopped or minced
seasoning
1 tbsp skimmed milk

Heat the oven to 200°C/400°F/gas 6.

Roll the pastry out thinly on a floured board and cut into six 10 cm/4 in circles. Melt the margarine. Add the onions and fry gently for 5 minutes. Stir in the carrot and stock and cook for about 5 minutes, or until most of the liquid has evaporated. Add the beans, sauces, meat and seasoning. Allow the mixture to cool then spoon on to 3 of the circles. Moisten the edges with water and top with the remaining circles. Seal and flute the edges. Brush with milk and make a small slit in the top. Bake for 20–25 minutes or until the pastry is crisp and brown.

Kidneys in red wine

Serves 4

Each serving: 310 kcal/1300 kJ, 40 g (4 units) carbohydrate, 7 g fibre, 20 g protein, 6 g fat

1 tbsp polyunsaturated oil
150 ml/¼ pt meat stock
2 medium-sized onions, chopped
1 medium-sized carrot, chopped
300 g/10½ oz lambs' kidneys, skinned, cored and sliced
2 tbsp wholemeal flour
100 ml/3½ fl oz dry red wine
200 g/7 oz butter beans, canned without sugar, or cooked beans (see pages 12–13)
piece of bay leaf
sprig of parsley
seasoning
300 g/10½ oz cooked long-grain brown rice, sprinkled with chopped fresh herbs (see page 14)

Salad
1 medium-sized onion, sliced into rings
3 medium-sized tomatoes, sliced

Heat the oil with a few spoonfuls of stock in a large saucepan and fry the onions and carrot until they start to brown. Add the kidneys and cook until they are brown. Add the remaining stock and bring to the boil.

Blend the flour with a little cold water, stir into the saucepan and return to the boil. Cook for a further few minutes or until thickened. Mix in the wine, beans, herbs and seasoning, and simmer for 20 minutes.

Serve surrounded by brown rice and accompanied by onion-and-tomato salad.

Chicken chasseur

Serves 4

Each serving: 170 kcal/710 kJ, 10 g (1 unit) carbohydrate, 3 g fibre, 16 g protein, 4 g fat

225 g/8 oz cooked chicken, roughly chopped
stock or water
1 large onion, finely chopped
4 medium-sized tomatoes, chopped
1 medium-sized green pepper, chopped
225 g/8 oz mushrooms, sliced
250 ml/9 fl oz dry white wine
seasoning
1 tbsp chopped parsley
1 tbsp chopped chervil
1 tbsp chopped tarragon
1 tsp polyunsaturated margarine

Heat the chicken thoroughly in a little stock or water. Place the onion, tomatoes, pepper and mushrooms in a non-stick saucepan with water and simmer for 5 minutes. Add the wine, seasoning, herbs and margarine and cook for a further 5 minutes, or until hot. With a slotted spoon, transfer the chicken to a hot serving dish and pour over the sauce.

Pizza baps

Makes 8 mini-pizzas (pizzette)
Each pizzetta: 130 kcal/550 kJ, 10 g (1 unit) carbohydrate, 3 g fibre, 8 g protein, 6 g fat

1 tbsp polyunsaturated margarine
100 g/3½ oz skimmed milk curd cheese
½ tsp dried oregano
½ tsp dried thyme
4 spring onions, finely chopped
4 tbsp mixed peppers
1 tsp paprika
4 wholemeal baps, split
60 g/2 oz lean cooked ham, sliced into strips
4 tbsp grated Gouda or Edam cheese
60 g/2 oz canned anchovies, drained
8 stuffed olives, sliced

Cream the margarine, curd cheese and herbs together and beat in the spring onions, peppers and paprika. Spread over the halved baps. Place slices of ham on top and sprinkle with the grated cheese. Arrange a lattice of anchovies on top, garnish with the sliced olives and cook under a hot grill until the cheese is golden brown. Serve with a salad (see pages 29–30). For children the sliced olives and anchovies can be made into a special design, such as a face or a house.

Mushroom and cauliflower au gratin

Serves 4
Each serving: 250 kcal/1050 kJ, 20 g (2 units) carbohydrate, 9 g fibre, 22 g protein, 9 g fat

115 g/4 oz lean cooked ham, chopped
200 g/7 oz mushrooms, chopped
100 g/3½ oz cooked wholemeal spaghetti in 2.5 cm/1 in lengths (see page 15)
2 tsp Worcester sauce
500 ml/18 fl oz Thin Pouring Sauce (see page 99)
1 hard-boiled egg, chopped
3 tbsp chopped parsley
1 medium-sized cauliflower, cut into sprigs
6 tbsp wholemeal breadcrumbs
seasoning

Add the ham, mushrooms, spaghetti and Worcester sauce to the pouring sauce and simmer for 10 minutes. Stir in the egg and most of the parsley.

Meanwhile, cook the cauliflower in boiling salted water until tender, drain and put into a flat dish. Pour the hot sauce over and sprinkle with the breadcrumbs, pressing them into the mixture slightly. Brown under a moderately hot grill. Sprinkle the remainder of the parsley on top before serving.

Savoury Spaghetti with Chick Peas (top, see p. 104), Pizza Baps (bottom).

Alternatively, the dish can be prepared in advance, covered and stored in the refrigerator, then cooked in a moderately hot oven (200°C/400°F/gas 6) for about 30 minutes.

Italian crispy vegetables

Serves 4

Each serving: 240 kcal/1010 kJ, 30 g (3 units) carbohydrate, 10 g fibre, 12 protein, 8 g fat

1 medium-sized onion, chopped
1 clove garlic, crushed
2 tbsp mixed chopped peppers
4 medium-sized tomatoes, chopped
1 small aubergine, cut into thin slices with skin
4 tbsp cooked fresh or frozen peas
4 tbsp cooked cannellini or other beans (see pages 12–13)
1 tbsp polyunsaturated oil
seasoning
2 eggs, beaten
4 large, medium-cut slices wholemeal bread, toasted

Salad

100 g/3½ oz cucumber, sliced with skin
100 g/3½ oz radishes, sliced
100 g/3½ oz spring onions, sliced
100 g/3½ oz red cabbage, shredded

Cook the vegetables in the oil for 15–20 minutes, stirring occasionally. Remove from the heat, add seasoning and eggs and cook gently, stirring, until the eggs are just set. Cut the toast slices in half diagonally, place overlapping on a hot serving dish and pour over the vegetable and egg mixture. Accompany with individual bowls of different-coloured salad vegetables.

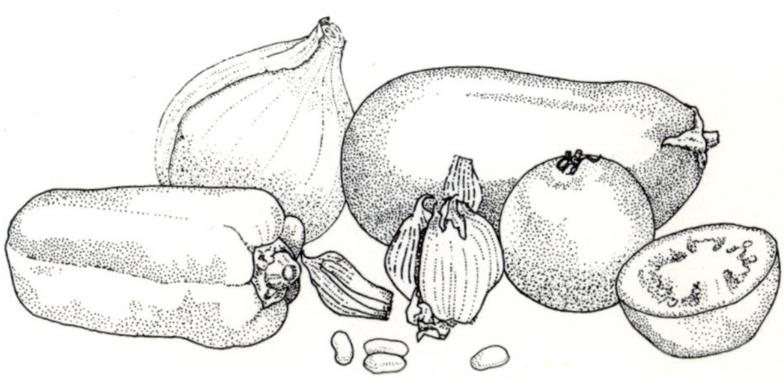

Havana Rice and Black Beans (top left, see p. 103), Italian Crispy Vegetables (centre right), Tuna and Anchovy Quiche (bottom, see p. 105).

Oxford muesli

Each 60 g/2 oz (6 tbsp) serving: 170 kcal/710 kJ, 30 g (3 units) carbohydrate, 13 g fibre, 6 g protein, 4 g fat

60 g/2 oz rolled oats
60 g/2 oz cracked wheat
60 g/2 oz barley flakes
60 g/2 oz rye flakes
60 g/2 oz large natural bran flakes
60 g/2 oz All-Bran
60 g/2 oz soya bran
60 g/2 oz dried apricots, chopped
60 g/2 oz mixed raisins, currants and sultanas, chopped
60 g/2 oz hazelnuts, ground or finely chopped
¼ tsp mixed spice

Mix all the ingredients together and store in an airtight container. Serve with milk, low-fat plain yoghurt, yoghurt juice (sugar-free) or fresh fruit sweetened with a sugar-free sweetener if liked.

DAILY MEAL PLANS

The following meal plan suggestions use recipes from this book:

1000 kcal/4200 kJ diet

A day's meals using recipes in this book

Daily:	300 ml/½ pt skimmed milk for coffee and tea
Breakfast:	90 g/9 stewed dried apricots halves 1 wholemeal bread roll 1 tsp polyunsaturated margarine 1 tsp sugar-free diabetic marmalade Coffee or tea
Midmorning:	Coffee or tea
Midday:	Beans and Mushrooms (see page 35) Summer Fruit Salad (see page 87)
Afternoon:	Coffee or tea
Evening:	Turkey and Pasta Salad (see page 28) 1 small thin-cut slice wholemeal bread 1 tsp polyunsaturated margarine Raspberry Yoghurt Pudding (see page 85)
Bedtime:	Coffee or tea using remainder of daily milk allowance 1 Ginger Square (see page 83)

1200 kcal/5040 kJ diet

A day's meals using recipes in this book

Daily:	450 ml/¾ pt skimmed milk for coffee, tea and cereal
Breakfast:	1 small banana, sliced 3 tbsp Oxford Muesli (see page 112) 1 small thin-cut slice of wholemeal bread, toasted 1 tsp polyunsaturated margarine 1 tsp sugar-free diabetic marmalade Coffee or tea
Midmorning:	Coffee or tea
Midday:	Tuna, Chick Pea and Pasta Salad (see page 27) 1 wholemeal crispbread 1 tsp polyunsaturated margarine Fromage Blanc and Fruit (see page 86)
Afternoon:	Coffee or tea
Evening:	Mexican Chicken (see page 46) 6 tbsp long-grain brown rice Haricots verts Strawberry Sorbet (see page 89)
Bedtime:	Coffee or tea using remainder of daily milk allowance 1 Oatmeal Finger (see page 96)

1500 kcal/6300 kJ diet

A day's meals using recipes in this book

Daily:	600 ml/1 pt skimmed milk for coffee, tea and cereal
Breakfast:	1 small glass (7 tbsp) fresh orange juice 125 g/4½ oz porridge 1 wholemeal bread roll 1 tsp polyunsaturated margarine 1 tsp sugar-free diabetic marmalade Coffee or tea
Midmorning:	Coffee or tea 2 Wholemeal Savoury Biscuits (see page 96)
Midday:	Scottish Lentil Broth (see page 20) 60 g/2 oz Seafood Pâté (see page 20) 3 wholemeal rye crispbreads 2 tsp polyunsaturated margarine Sliced tomatoes
Afternoon:	Coffee or tea 1 Country Square (see page 93)
Evening:	Steak and Kidney Hot-Pot (see page 49) Peas and carrots 2 small boiled new potatoes, tossed in parsley Blackberry and Apple Crunchie (see page 87)
Bedtime:	Coffee or tea, using remainder of daily milk allowance 2 Wholemeal Orange Biscuits (see page 95)

2000 kcal/8400 kJ diet

A day's meals using recipes in this book

Daily:	600 ml/1 pt skimmed milk for coffee, tea and cereal
Breakfast:	½ fresh grapefruit 2 Weetabix 1 large medium-cut slice wholemeal bread, toasted 1 tsp polyunsaturated margarine 1 tsp sugar-free diabetic marmalade Coffee or tea
Midmorning:	Coffee or tea 2 Popovers with Dates (see page 97)
Midday:	1 Savoury Beef Pasty (see page 106) Potato and Bean Salad (see page 30) Coleslaw with Apple (see page 29) 1 pear
Afternoon:	Coffee or tea 2 Buttermilk Scones (see page 97) 2 tsp polyunsaturated margarine 1 tsp sugar-free diabetic jam
Evening:	Chicken and Celery Soup (see page 18) Sausage Risotto (see page 105) Caribbean Baked Bananas (see page 84)
Bedtime:	Coffee or tea using remainder of daily milk allowance 2 Biscuits with Sesame Seeds (see page 98) 1 piece of fruit

2500 kcal/10500 kJ diet

A day's meals using recipes in this book

Daily:	600 ml/1 pt skimmed milk for coffee, tea and cereal
Breakfast:	60 g/2 oz Oxford Muesli (see page 112) 1 wholemeal bread roll 1 tsp polyunsaturated margarine 1 tsp sugar-free diabetic marmalade Coffee or tea
Midmorning:	Coffee or tea 1 slice of Fruit Cake (see page 62)
Midday:	Lentils with Tomatoes (see page 36) 1 apple, or other piece of fruit
Afternoon:	Coffee or tea 2 Fruit Scones (see page 98) 2 tsp polyunsaturated margarine
Evening:	Italian Lamb Casserole (see page 53) 50 g/1¾ oz crusty wholemeal bread 1 glass dry red wine Loganberry Cheesecake (see page 86)
Bedtime:	Coffee or tea using remainder of daily milk allowance 2 halves Pizza Baps (see page 110)

Acknowledgements

We would like to thank the following for their help in the preparation of this book: David Cunningham, FHCI, MRSH, for his work as catering consultant; Honor Runciman, SRD, for market research; Susan Lousley, BSc (Hons), SRD, for computer analysis; Anne Reeve and Grace Seccombe for typing the manuscript.

Most of the food analysis figures are based on *McCance and Widdowson's The Composition of Foods* (4th rev ed) by A. A. Paul and D. A. T. Southgate; and *Food Composition Tables for Use in East Asia* by the Food and Agriculture Organization. Additional food analysis was supplied by Dr D. A. T. Southgate and Dr Anne Walker. Granose Foods Ltd supplied the soya bran analysis.

Roberta Longstaff and Jim Mann, 1984

The publishers are grateful to the following organizations for their assistance with the photography: Pasta Foods Ltd for supplying the pasta; and David Mellor Ltd, 4 Sloane Square, London, SW1, for providing the salad bowls on page 23.

The photographs were taken by Peter Myers, assisted by Neil Mersh. Art direction was by Rose and Lamb Design Partnership, styling by Alison Williams, and food preparation by Jane Suthering.

The line drawings are by Sue Rose.

INDEX TO RECIPES

Page numbers in *italic* refer to the illustrations.

Positive Health Guides published in 1984

EYES: THEIR PROBLEMS AND TREATMENTS

Michael Glasspool, FRCS

A renowned consultant ophthalmic surgeon tells you all you need to know about the many conditions that can affect your eyes – from squints and conjunctivitis to cataracts and glaucoma.

OVERCOMING DYSLEXIA

A straightforward guide for families and teachers

Dr Bevé Hornsby

'This easy-to-read book is optimistic and full of practical advice, and in my opinion no teacher or parent of a dyslexic child should be without it.'

Susan Hampshire

ACNE

Advice on clearing your skin

Prof Ronald Marks

This eminent professor of dermatology gives practical advice on what factors to avoid, which are the most effective remedies you can buy and how you should use them.

CONQUERING PAIN

How to overcome the discomfort of arthritis, backache, migraine, heart disease, childbirth, period pain and many other common conditions

Dr Sampson Lipton

THE MENOPAUSE

Coping with the change

Dr Jean Coope

A well-woman counsellor shows how you can make the menopause a change for the better.

Other Positive Health Guides

THE BACK – RELIEF FROM PAIN
Patterns of back pain – how to deal with and avoid them

Dr Alan Stoddard

STRESS AND RELAXATION
Jane Madders

BEAT HEART DISEASE!
A cardiologist explains how you can help your heart and enjoy a healthier life

Prof Risteard Mulcahy

OVERCOMING ARTHRITIS
A guide to coping with stiff or aching joints

Dr Frank Dudley Hart

PSORIASIS
A guide to one of the commonest skin diseases

Prof Ronald Marks

ASTHMA & HAY FEVER
How to relieve wheezing and sneezing

Dr Allan Knight

VARICOSE VEINS
How they are treated, and what you can do to help

Prof Harold Ellis

HIGH BLOOD PRESSURE
What is means for you, and how to control it

Dr Eoin O'Brien and Prof Kevin O'Malley

MIGRAINE AND HEADACHES
Understanding, avoiding and controlling the pain

Dr Marcia Wilkinson

DON'T FORGET FIBRE IN YOUR DIET
To help avoid many of our commonest diseases

Dr Denis Burkitt

THE HIGH-FIBRE COOKBOOK
Recipes for good health

Pamela Westland
Introduced by Denis Burkitt

GET A BETTER NIGHT'S SLEEP
Prof Ian Oswald and Dr Kirstine Adam

ECZEMA AND DERMATITIS
How to cope with inflamed skin

Prof Rona MacKie

ENJOY SEX IN THE MIDDLE YEARS
Dr Christine E. Sandford

ANXIETY & DEPRESSION
A practical guide to recovery

Prof Robert Priest